Attacking Football Defenses

with

RADAR BLOCKING

by

Leo Hand

Parker Publishing Company, Inc.
West Nyack, New York

DEDICATION

The quest to find football's "perfect blocking system" ended in success only because I was constantly supported by a lovely lady and three wonderful children who not only understood my obsession, but made great personal sacrifices to help make Radar Blocking a reality. This book is fondly dedicated to my wife Beth and our three children, Mary Beth, Michael and David.

© 1985 *by*

PARKER PUBLISHING COMPANY, INC.

West Nyack, N.Y.

Library of Congress Cataloging in Publication Data

Hand, Leo
   Attacking football defenses with radar blocking.

   Includes index.
   1. Football—Offense. 2. Blocking (Football)
3. Football—Coaching. I. Title
GV951.8.H26 1984   796.332'2   84-22643

ISBN 0-13-050220-0

Printed in the United States of America

Why Another Football Book?

Some men see things as they are and say why. I dream things that never were and say why not.

Robert F. Kennedy

When I began coaching 15 years ago, I attempted to teach my players pretty much the same basic things that I had been taught by my former coaches. I was fortunate in that I had played for some very outstanding men and most of the things I had learned were sound and progressive. When it came to teaching my offensive linemen who to block, however, I gradually began to feel inadequate. As a player, I had learned the Split-T numbering system and at the onset of my career, I thought that this would be a great system to use. It is both simple and easy to teach. The more I became involved with X's and O's, however, the more I realized that the numbering system did not adapt well to multiple blocking schemes, nor was it truly an inclusive system. Because of these shortcomings, I began to search for a better system.

I began my research by investigating professional literature. In a short time I had read almost every text that had ever been written on the subject of football coaching. I also attended a multitude of coaching clinics. During these early years, my telephone bills were outrageous. I literally spent thousands of dollars calling every college and professional coach in the nation who would discuss this matter with me. My efforts were in vain and my frustrations grew progressively worse. There simply wasn't a "perfect" blocking system yet in existence. Because I had asked the question "Why not?", I felt compelled to develop one.

Radar blocking is a rather inadequate term that I have selected to describe the results of my efforts. The component principles of the Radar system are not entirely original. I doubt that any coach in today's game could claim total originality for any innovative twist. Innovations in modern football result because of successful attempts to synthesize and refine existing principles of sound fundamental play. Radar blocking is a cumulative effort that was achieved only because of the vast contributions of others.

3

Simply defined, Radar blocking is a consolidation of football's finest blocking systems. Radar assignments are inclusive, concise directives that enable offensive linemen to block every conceivable defensive variation. The Radar system nullifies any defensive attempt to surprise an offensive team with an unanticipated defense. Even if an offensive team has never practiced against a particular defense, its players will have absolutely no difficulty adapting their Radar assignments to it.

Furthermore, since the Radar system is comprehensive, there is no need for a coach to toil each week preparing an offensive game plan. Once a coach selects a series of Radar Master Calls (blocking schemes), his team has an intrinsic plan for attacking *every* defense. With the Radar system, offensive planning involves a one-shot, sequential coordination of Master Calls with offensive formations, backfield maneuvers and pass routes. Since this book offers a multitude of valuable suggestions as to how this may be accomplished, its scope exceeds Radar blocking. Although the book offers countless methods of enhancing offensive efficiency, no attempt is made to advocate the merits of any particular offensive system. Instead, this book suggests ways of making any offense a more dynamic, explosive attack.

Attacking Football Defenses with Radar Blocking is written in direct, simple language. Much of the material has been organized into a playbook type format. This organization will provide you with a quick, easy reference source for many years to come. I once heard John McKay remark that his favorite play was the "pitch play"—the play where one of his players "pitches" the ball to the referee after he crosses the goal line. I sincerely hope that this book not only stimulates your offensive thinking, but enables your team to consistently execute football's most exciting play—the "pitch play."

Leo Hand

ACKNOWLEDGMENTS

My deep thanks and appreciation to the following individuals who are really a part of this book.

To my high school and college coaches: Bill Guerrera, Jack Harten, Frank "Hunk" Vadas, Ron Blaylock, Al Kouneski, John McVey and George Perles, who taught me that football can be both challenging and fun.

To my early bosses, Tom Seymour, Bob Rosmarino and Joe Repko, who patiently tolerated my impatience.

To the finest coaches I know, my former associate coaches: Mike Piehler, Steve Cappic, Maurice Valentine, Stirling Hart, Bob Walker, Bob Peters, Roger Ramos and Bob Hand.

To a very courageous Athletic Director, Terry Mathews.

To my dear friend and the best high school Principal in the world, Father Les Esposito.

To Wayne Howard and his Long Beach City College staff: Andy Anderson, Ken Gregory, Don Klopenburg, Glen McFarland, Earl McCullouch, Jim Murphy, Will Shaw and Gary "Jake" Jacobsen.

To all the wonderful young men who it has been my good fortune to have coached.

But most of all, to Ma and Pa, who insisted that I get a college education and made tremendous sacrifices to help me achieve this goal.

L.H.

TABLE OF CONTENTS

1

Investigating
the Evolution of
Radar Blocking

It is extremely difficult, time-consuming and somewhat frustrating to devise a system of blocking assignments that will adequately handle the multitude of defensive alignments that are presently in vogue. Despite the problems involved in formulating such a system, however, the fact still remains that it is the coach's job to teach his players not only *how* to block, but also *who* to block. Any coach who sends his players into a game with inadequate, or non-existent blocking assignments is simply not doing his job.

In order for a blocking system to be truly effective, it must possess four distinctive characteristics:

1. Enables players to ascertain the location of their assignment prior to the snap of the ball.
2. Possesses the capability of effectively blocking stunts, by being flexible enough to allow players to switch assignments at the snap of the ball.
3. Is simple enough to insure the feasibility of its implementation.
4. Is comprehensive enough to guarantee that linemen will not be caught off-guard by an unanticipated, surprise defense.

Radar blocking is the only system I know of that possesses all four of these characteristics.

9

The purpose of this chapter is to examine some of the more traditional blocking systems of the past in an attempt to show how the Radar system has evolved by incorporating the strengths of these systems and rejecting their weaknesses.

DEFENSIVE RECOGNITION

Defensive recognition is probably the oldest, but least effective method of teaching blocking assignments. This system requires offensive linemen to recognize the defensive front and then remember which defender they are assigned to block. Back in the days when players sported handlebar moustaches and leather helmets, playing on the offensive line was a very uncomplicated affair. Coaches had not yet invented enough defensive alignments or offensive maneuvers to complicate the job of the "Seven Blocks of Granite." Defensive recognition was thus a very feasible and effective method of teaching a player who to block.

Because of the defensive and offensive innovations that have taken place throughout the years, however, defensive recognition has become an obsolete system. For every blocking scheme employed, today's offensive linemen must be given an instrument that will enable them to remember their blocking assignment versus 11 to 15 different defensive sets. An offensive guard, for example, must remember his assignment versus at least 15 different defensive sets. Offensive centers and tackles must know their assignments versus at least 13 sets, and the tight end must be prepared to block 11 different sets. (See Figures 1-1A,B,C and D.) Even if a team was very conservative and limited its entire attack to a total of seven or eight (run and pass) blocking schemes, offensive linemen who had to rely on defensive recognition, would be required to memorize more than 100 different blocking assignments! Obviously, this is impossible.

The few coaches who still use defensive recognition never attempt to teach their players to block every defensive set. Instead, they teach assignments for the most commonly used defenses (example: odd, even and gap) and then adjust blocking assignments against opponents who vary from the norm. There is a great deal of risk involved in this approach. Surprise has always been an effective element in football strategy, and when such a team is surprised by a new defense that they have never practiced against the results can be devastating.

Radar blocking is built on the premise that offensive linemen should be prepared to block every defense—even those that it has never practiced against. Defensive recognition is thus not one of the philosophies incorporated into the Radar system.

THE SPLIT-T NUMBERING SYSTEM

One of the simplest blocking systems ever devised was the old Split-T numbering system. In this system, any defender playing over the center is numbered 0 and the remaining defenders along the line of scrimmage are numbered in

Figure 1-1

Center Sets 1-1A

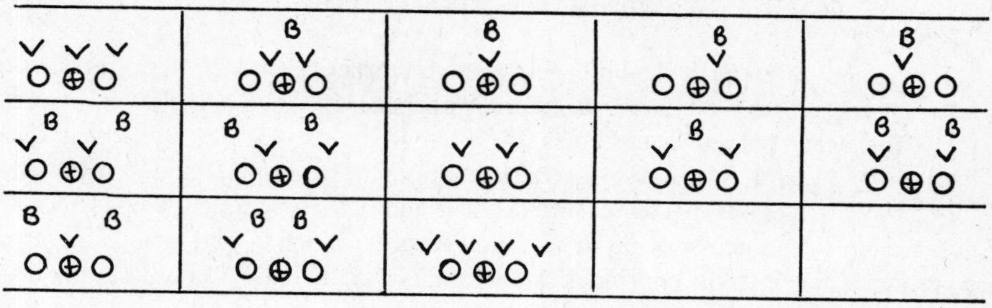

Guard Sets 1-1B

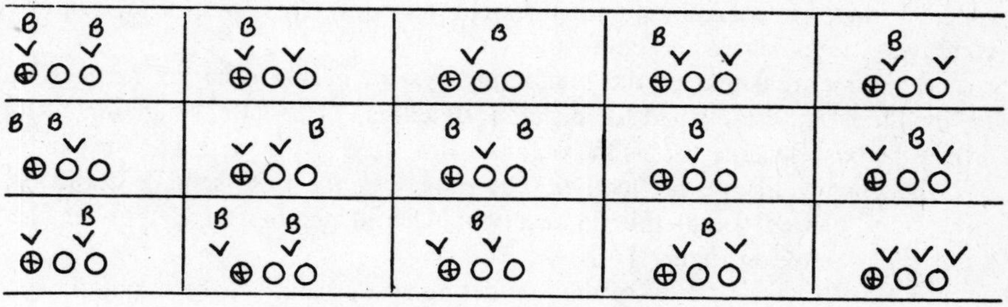

Tackle Sets 1-1C

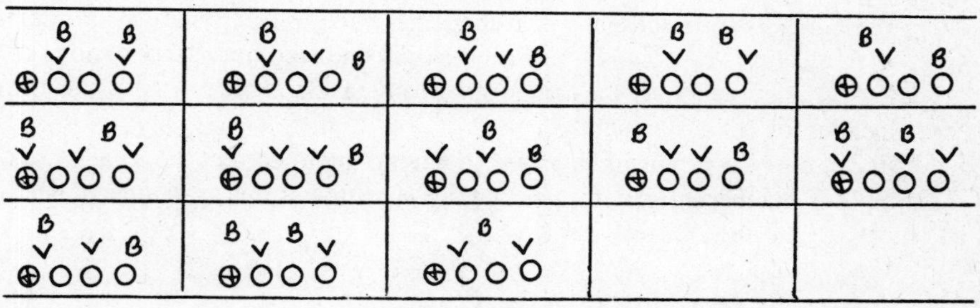

End Sets 1-1D

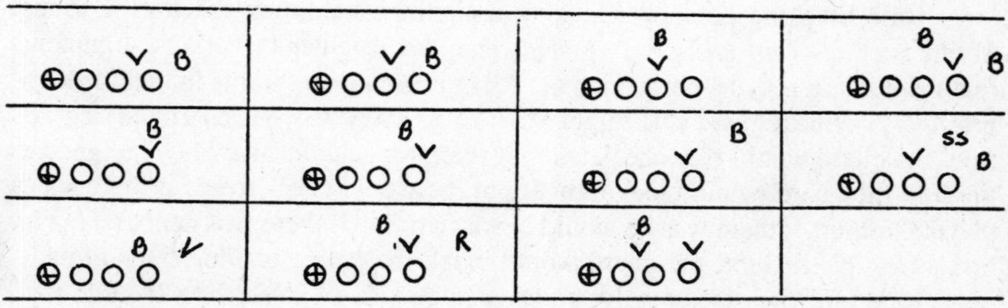

progression 1,2,3,4, etc. (Figure 1-2). Offensive linemen are then assigned to block a specific number. For example, the center blocks 0, the guard blocks 1, the tackle blocks 2 and the tight end blocks 3. (This is referred to as base blocking.)

Although the Split-T numbering system worked well with the Split-T offense, it does contain a number of inherent weaknesses which make it ineffective for many other offensive systems. The first of these weaknesses is that the numbering system is not sophisticated enough to accommodate a variety of blocking schemes. Consider a simple slant play, for example. Versus a 3-4 defense the assignments would be as follows: center-block 0, guard-pull and trap 3, tackle-block 2, tight end-block 1 (Figure 1-3A). If these same assignments were applied to the Split-4 defense, however, the play would be a total disaster (Figure 1-3B). The only way that a coach can compensate for this problem is to establish different assignments for different defenses. This, of course, can become very complicated and confusing.

Another weakness of the numbering system is that different numbering systems must be established for different defenses. If the offense attempted to utilize the base scheme versus the defense illustrated in Figure 1-4A, for example, the play would be ineffective. The only way the base scheme could be effectively utilized versus this defense would be to number the defense in the manner illustrated in Figure 1-4B.

Two other weaknesses of the numbering system are: (1) Stemming defensive fronts can drive offensive linemen crazy, since they must continuously renumber the defense; (2) Offensive linemen must be aware of what is happening along the entire line of scrimmage, rather than being able to zero in on their specific area. This is especially tough on the tight end who must be conscious of the defensive alignment over the center, guard and tackle in order to ascertain the exact location of his assignment.

Because of the problems involved in attempting to correct the weaknesses of the Split-T numbering system, none of the elements of this system have been incorporated into the Radar system.

RULE BLOCKING

Rule blocking conveys blocking assignments through the use of terms. Terms such as *Gap*, *On*, *Over*, *Inside*, and *Outside*, depict various alignments that the defense may be positioned in. Assignments group terms in their order of priority. A typical guard rule might read: Gap, On, Over. When employing this rule, the guard would first check *Gap*. If there was a defensive player aligned in the *Gap* the guard would block him. If not, he would check to see if there was a player *On* him. If there was he would block him, but if there was neither a player in his *Gap* or *On* him, the guard would block the player playing *Over* him.

Rule blocking does require a player to be able to associate a specific term with a specific defensive alignment. It also requires that the player memorize his

Figure 1-2

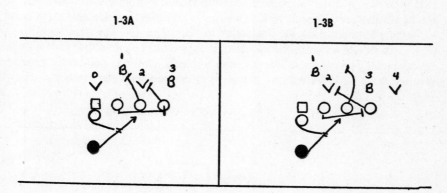

Figure 1-3

1-3A

1-3B

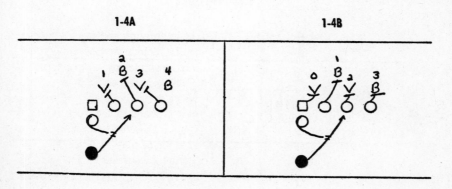

Figure 1-4

1-4A

1-4B

assignment, but once these skills have been mastered, the player will be able to locate his assignment against every defense—even those that he has never practiced against. Another advantage of the system is that rule assignments are fairly simple and easy to learn. The main weakness of rule blocking is that it is not flexible enough to accommodate defensive stunts. Once an offensive lineman locates his assigned defender he must attempt to block him—no matter what the defender does after the ball is hiked.

ZONE BLOCKING

Zone blocking begins by defining various zones along the line of scrimmage. Because each offense is different, coaches zone the line of scrimmage differently to fulfill the specific needs of their offense. Figure 1-5 illustrates three different methods of zoning. Like rule assignments, zone assignments are also prioritized. A typical guard's zone assignment might read: "Zone 1, Zone 2, Zone 2 LB." When employing this assignment, the guard would first check Zone 1. If there was a defensive lineman playing in this area he would block him, if not, he would check Zone 2. If there was not a defensive lineman aligned in Zone 2, the guard would block the linebacker in Zone 2.

Like rule blocking, zone blocking is an inclusive system that does a great job of teaching an offensive lineman *who* to block. Unfortunately, both systems have the same basic weakness—neither is effective versus the stunt.

Figure 1-5

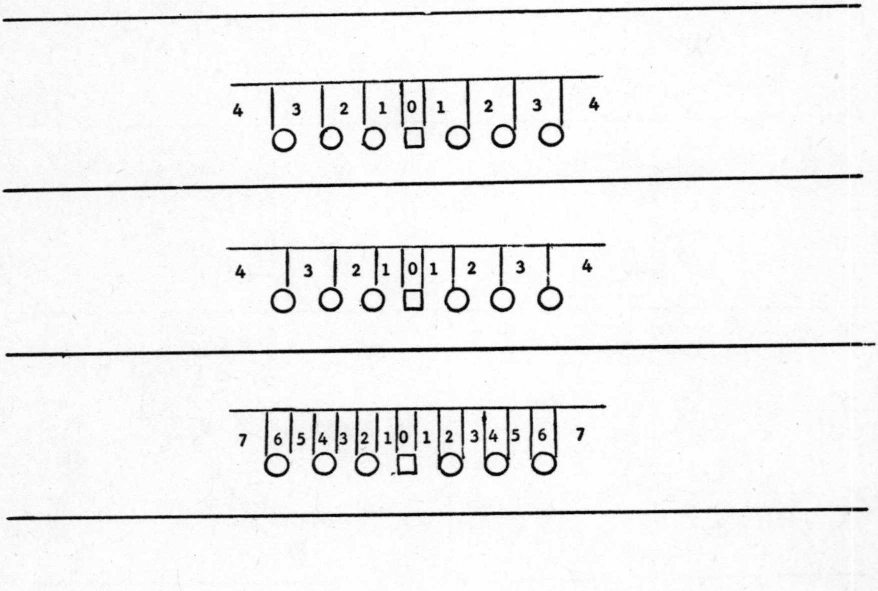

CALL BLOCKING

Call blocking is one of the most exciting innovations to come along in recent years. The system is characterized by blocking calls that are made at the line of scrimmage by the players themselves. Calls are made for various reasons, and each coach seems to have his own variety of calls. No matter which calls a coach may have his players employ, however, all blocking calls fit into one of two categories. They are either master calls or else they are combo calls.

Master calls communicate a specific blocking scheme to the entire offensive line or to one side of the line. Master calls are usually set up to afford a team the luxury of utilizing a single backfield maneuver with multiple blocking schemes. Figure 1-6 illustrates eight different master calls that could be used to enhance the effectiveness of the fullback off-tackle play.

Figure 1-6

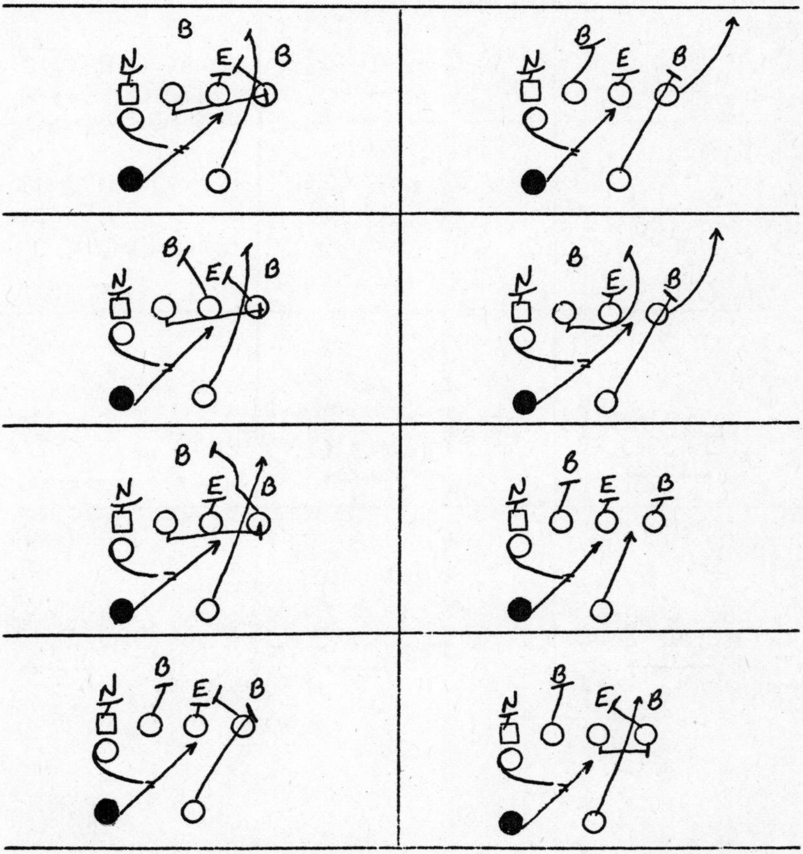

Combo calls involve two players. Two very important reasons why players make combo calls are: (1) To swap assignments for the purpose of gaining a leverage or angle advantage over the defense; (2) To alert one another to the possibility of a stunt, thus insuring that both players employ techniques that will enable them to correctly block the stunt. Figure 1-7 illustrates 12 of the most common combo calls in use today.

Call blocking is not in itself a blocking system. It does not tell an offensive player who to block, but it does add a missing dimension to a blocking system. When call blocking is consolidated with a sound traditional blocking system, a dynamic package is created. I call this package Radar blocking.

Figure 1-7

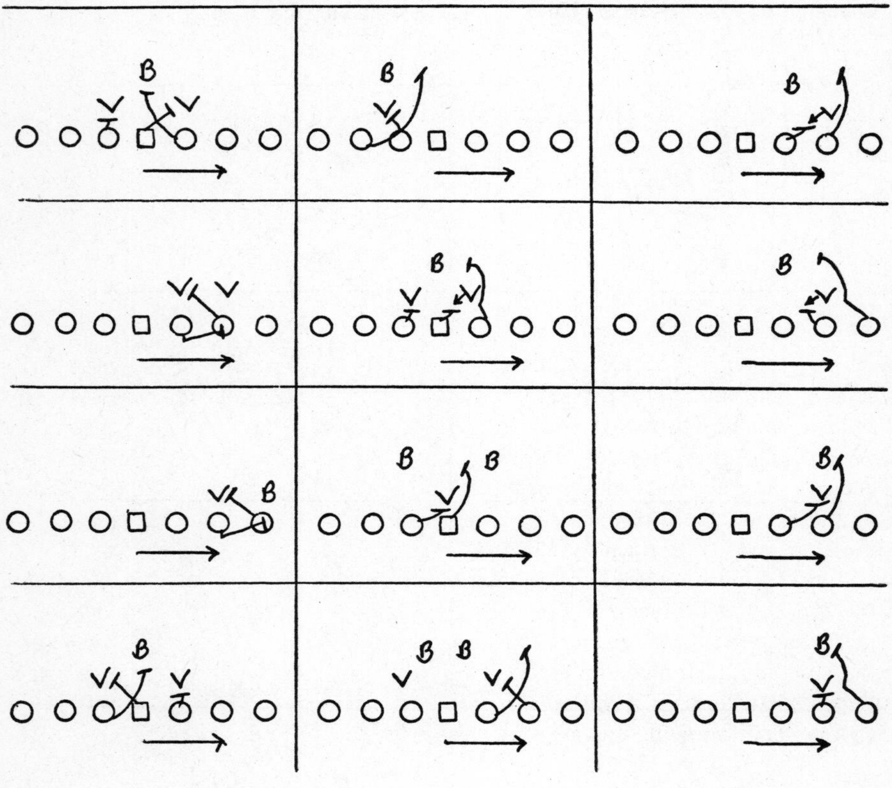

2

Radar Blocking—
A Consolidation of
Rule and Call Blocking

Throughout the years offensive line coaches have attempted to devise a trenchant, yet simple and flexible, system that teaches their players who to block. Defensive recognition, the Split-T numbering system, the "Maze," rule blocking, zone blocking and call blocking are all examples of this effort. As time has passed, most of these systems have gone through an evolution that usually refines them through the introduction of innovative ideas, or by consolidating them with other systems.

Radar blocking is a term that describes the consolidation and refinement of both rule and call blocking. Rule blocking provides the system with inclusive, exact assignments that enable a coach to engineer his offense against virtually every defense. Call blocking provides flexibility. It enables offensive linemen to attack the defense in a variety of ways, utilizing the best possible blocking scheme. The following are some of the advantages of Radar blocking:

1. Because rule assignments adapt to every defense:
   A. Little time is needed to prepare a weekly game plan. The implementation of a series of sequential master calls assures a permanent game plan.
   B. A team can never be caught off-guard by a surprise defense.
   C. Coaches need not waste valuable time continuously reteaching players who to block each week. This affords a team additional time to perfect blocking techniques.

17

2. Combo blocking calls make the offensive line impenetrable versus stunting defenses.

3. Master blocking calls enable a team to utilize one backfield action with numerous blocking schemes.

RULE BLOCKING NOMENCLATURE

Rule blocking conveys blocking assignments through the use of terms. Terms such as Gap, On, Over and Inside depict various alignments that the defense may be positioned in. Rule assignments group terms in their order of priority. A typical guard assignment might read: "Gap, On, Over." When employing this assignment, the guard would simply progress through the priority of these terms until he encounters a defender aligned in one of these positions. The following are the terms used in the Radar system:

1. *Attackside and Backside:* Attackside refers to the side of the line to which the play is being run. The backside is the side of the line away from the point of attack. The center is neither backside nor attackside (Figure 2-1).

2. *Gap:* Refers to any defensive lineman aligned between two offensive linemen. The Gap rule for both the attackside and backside linemen is always toward the ball and the center's Gap rule is always toward the attackside (Fig. 2-2A). When a defensive lineman is aligned on the inside crotch of the tight end, tackle or guard, he is also considered to be in the Gap (Fig. 2-2B). When the defense is in a "Split" alignment, the inside linebackers and tackles are also considered to be in the Gap (Fig. 2-2C).

3. *On and Over:* On depicts defensive *linemen* who are aligned head up or outside shade with an offensive lineman (Fig. 2-3A). Over refers to *linebackers* (Fig. 2-3B).

4. *Linebacker:* Instructs an offensive lineman to block the most dangerous linebacker away from the point of attack. Thus if the play is directed to the right and a player is assigned Linebacker, he will block the most dangerous linebacker to his left (Fig. 2-4).

5. *Inside and Outside:* Inside means that an offensive lineman is assigned to block any defender playing in his Gap or On the next offensive lineman to his inside (Fig. 2-5 A and B). Outside is the exact opposite of Inside (Fig. 2-5 C and D).

Figure 2-1

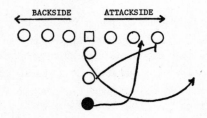

Figure 2-2

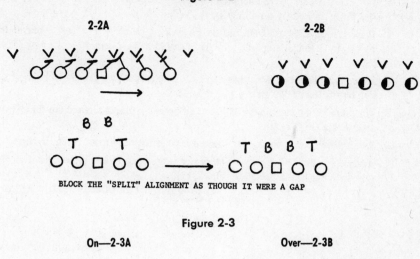

2-2A

2-2B

B B

T   T   T B B T

BLOCK THE "SPLIT" ALIGNMENT AS THOUGH IT WERE A GAP

Figure 2-3

On—2-3A   Over—2-3B

Figure 2-4

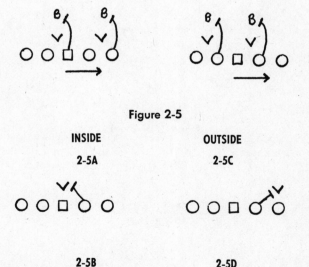

Figure 2-5

INSIDE   OUTSIDE

2-5A   2-5C

2-5B   2-5D

6. *Fill:* Tells an offensive lineman to block any defender aligned in the area that has been vacated by a pulling lineman (Fig. 2-6).

7. *Backside Gap:* Is assigned mostly on passing plays. It instructs a player to block any defender aligned in the gap away from the direction of the play (Fig. 2-7).

8. *Hunt:* Is assigned only on passing plays. It instructs a player to block the most dangerous linebacker in his area (Fig. 2-8).

9. *Tandem:* Refers to a linebacker stacked behind a player aligned On the offensive tackle (Fig. 2-9).

10. *Stack:* Refers to a linebacker stacked behind the nose tackle (Fig. 2-10).

11. *Away:* (For the center only.) The center is assigned to block the most dangerous defender to the backside (Fig. 2-11).

Figure 2-6—Fill

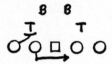

Figure 2-7—Backside Gap

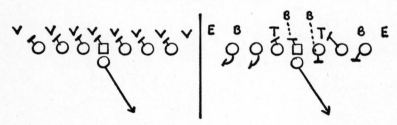

Figure 2-8—Hunt

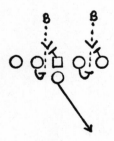

Figure 2-9—Tandem

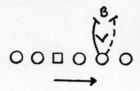

Figure 2-10—Stack

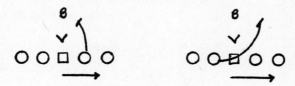

Figure 2-11—Away

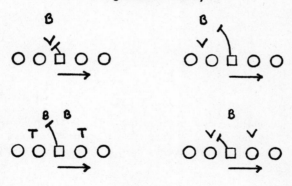

12. *Reach:* (For the attackside guard only.) The guard is assigned to block any defender in his outside gap (Fig. 2-12).

13. *Eagle:*(For the attackside end only.) The end is instructed to block:

   A. Any player in his Gap (Fig. 2-13A).

   B. Any player On or Over him whenever there is another defender outside of him playing on or near the line (Fig. 2-13B).

   C. Any player On him when he is confronted by a stack (Fig. 2-13C).

   D. A Tandem linebacker (Fig. 2-13D).

14. *Rule:* Means that the offensive lineman is assigned to block according to the following priority: Gap, On, Over, Linebacker.

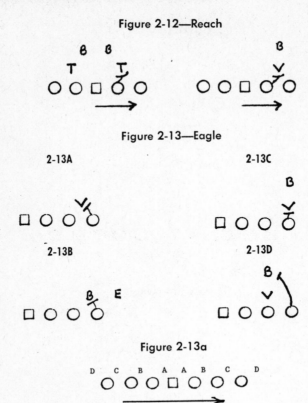

Figure 2-12—Reach

Figure 2-13—Eagle

2-13A

2-13C

2-13B

2-13D

Figure 2-13a

15. *Note:* Radar blocking also utilizes such terms as Downfield, Pull and Lead, Pull and Trap, but since these terms are self-explanatory, no definitions are needed. Reference is also frequently made to the universal gap lettering system.

COMBO CALLS

Radar blocking calls are divided into two categories. They are either master calls or combo calls. Master calls communicate a specific blocking scheme to the entire offensive line. Combo calls, on the other hand, involve only two players. They are optional and called at the line of scrimmage by the players themselves. Two very important reasons why players make combo calls are: (1) To swap assignments for the purpose of gaining a leverage or angle advantage over the defense; (2) To alert one another to the possibility of a stunt, thus insuring that both players employ techniques that will enable them to correctly block the stunt. Radar blocking utilizes four basic combo calls. These are:

1. *Crossblock:* A crossblock can be called by two offensive linemen or by an offensive lineman and a wingback or a slotback. There are three reasons why a crossblock might be desirable. The first reason is to divide two defensive

players at the point of attack. The only time that a crossblock would be used for this purpose is when the two players doing the crossblocking are confronted by defenders who are aligned in an On or Over position. Figure 2-14 illustrates four different crossblocks that divide defenders at the point of attack.

The second reason for crossblocking is to seal off either two attackside or two backside defenders. This is especially effective versus tandems or gap stack alignments. Four examples of this are shown in Figure 2-15.

The last reason for crossblocking is to slow down pursuit by confusing defensive reads. This tactic is only effective versus reading defenses. A good example of this is illustrated in Figure 2-16.

Figure 2-14

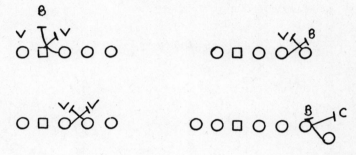

Figure 2-15

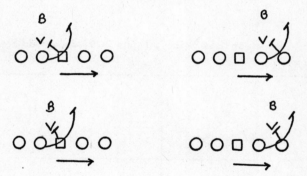

Figure 2-16

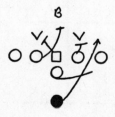

2. *Scoop:* This call is made between the backside guard and center. It is used versus odd defenses such as the 3-4 and 5-3. Its purpose is to cut off backside pursuit. An illustration of the techniques of scoop as they apply to the 3-4 defense is shown in Figure 2-17.

3. *Zone:* This is an attackside call that can be used versus odd or even sets. The call can be made between the center and the attackside guard (even), or between the attackside guard and tackle (odd). An illustration of zone techniques versus an even set is shown in Figure 2-18, and versus an odd set in Figure 2-19.

4. *Pop:* This is also an attackside call. It is used to attack stack, guard stack, tandem and end stack defenses (Fig. 2-20).

Figure 2-21 illustrates the Pop techniques that the attackside guard and tackle would use to block a guard stack set.

Figure 2-17—Scoop

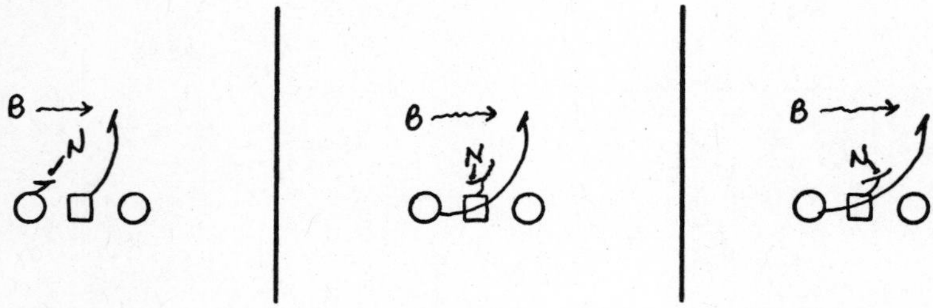

Figure 2-18—Zone (Even Set) 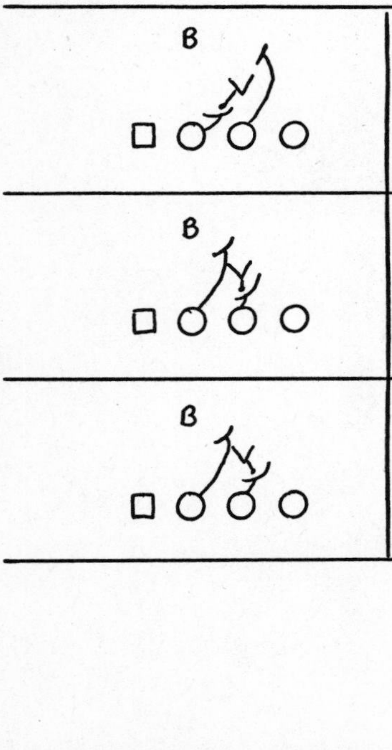   Figure 2-19—Zone (Odd Set)

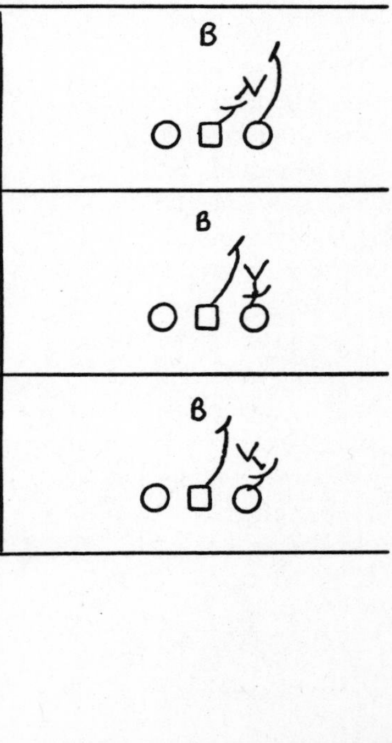

Figure 2-20

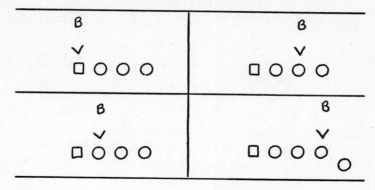

Figure 2-21—Pop

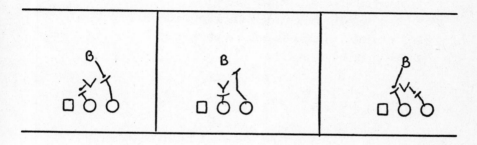

The system we utilize to implement our combo calls is extremely simple. We allow any offensive lineman who feels that he needs a better blocking angle or has the savvy to recognize a defensive weakness the freedom to make a combo call. On the other hand, if the player who the call man is requesting assistance from feels that a call may not be advantageous, he has the freedom to veto it. Let us say, for example, that the right guard desired to make a crossblock with the center and that the center's name was John. The right guard would simply say "John-X." (We use the letter X to communicate the word crossblock, but use the words Pop, Scoop and Zone to communicate those particular calls.) If the center also desired to crossblock he would reply "yes," but if he felt that a crossblock was not advantageous he could void it by replying "no." It should be noted that in reality, the players very infrequently have to make decisions regarding the use of combo calls. Providing that the defense does not suddenly vary from its normal pattern, offensive linemen instinctively know which combo calls are appropriate because they have been practicing them all week long.

MASTER CALLS

Master Call	
Word Priority Assignment	*Combo Calls*

A master call is a coordinated package that includes priority word assignments for the entire offensive line (Rule Blocking), along with possible combo calls (Call Blocking). A single master call can be used to engineer a single backfield action (Fig. 2-22), multiple backfield actions (Fig. 2-23), or a sequence of master calls can be established for a single backfield action (Fig. 2-24).

Master calls are divided into four categories. These are:

1. Master calls that attack the off-tackle hole.
2. Master calls that attack the inside sector of the defense.
3. Master calls that attack the perimeter of the defense.
4. Pass protection master calls.

Figure 2-22

Slant

Figure 2-23

If SLANT blocking is used for both backfield actions, one play would be a FB SLANT and the other a TB SLANT.

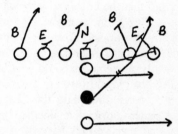

Figure 2-24

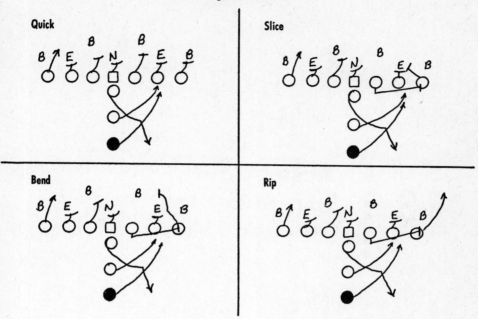

Occasionally a master call may have more than one use. Quick, for example, can be used to attack both the off-tackle hole and the inside sector.

Chapters 3 through 6 will present more than 30 different master calls. Obviously, no coach should attempt to use all of the master calls. It would be too confusing to his players. The reason why so many different master calls have been introduced is to give the reader a variety of choices. Enough master calls are presented to fulfill the needs of virtually every offense.

3

Master Calls
That Attack the
Off-Tackle Hole

Chapters 3, 4 and 5 will present the information necessary to implement the Radar Master Calls that are used to engineer the run offense. These chapters have been organized into a playbook-type format. It is hoped that this approach to organization is the most relevant and easily understood method of presenting this information to football coaches.

There are a number of concepts regarding the playbook format that should be explained in detail. First of all, each master call will be organized into a set of four illustrations. The first Figure in the set (Figure 3-3) will show the master call engineering an I formation play versus the 3-4 and 4-4 defenses. By selecting a specific formation (the I), the reader will see the development of a correlated sequence of blocking patterns and backfield actions. The reason that the 3-4 and 4-4 defenses have been selected for the initial presentation of the master call is because these are the most common seven- and eight-man defensive fronts in use today. Just below the illustrated play, there may or may not be (depending upon the master call), one or more suggested combo calls. The following is an example of how a combo call will be presented: "X: AST and ASG." This means that the attackside tackle and the attackside guard have the option of calling a crossblock versus the illustrated defense. Also in the first Figure (Figure 3-3) are "Comments and Coaching Points." These are remarks or suggestions that will help the reader better understand the purpose, uses and limitations of the master call.

The second Figure in the set (Figure 3-4) lists each player's blocking assignment, along with any combo calls that may be appropriate versus the illustrated defenses. It should be noted that although a combo call may be effective versus a particular variation of a defense, it may not be effective versus other variations of the same defense. As every experienced coach knows, there are a multitude of ways in which any one defense can be aligned. It is, therefore, important to understand that because there are so many different variations of a single defense, the combo calls that have been suggested for each defense are only applicable to that specific variation and may not be applicable to another variation of the same defense. Conversely, combo calls that have not been suggested for a particular variation of a defense may be very effective versus another variation of the same defense. An example of this concept is shown in Figure 3-1, A and B.

Figure 3-1

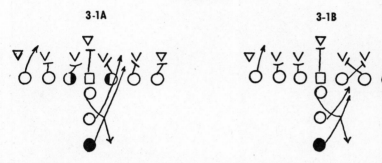

3-1A

3-1B

A guard-tackle crossblock is not feasible versus this variation of the 4-3 since it would be too difficult for the offensive tackle to block the defensive tackle.

But, a crossblock versus this variation of the 4-3 would be very effective.

The third Figure in the set of four illustrations (Figure 3-5) illustrates Radar assignments versus 12 different defenses. The left column illustrates seven-man fronts and the right column shows eight-man fronts and goal-line defenses. The reason why these particular defenses have been selected is because they offer the reader an overview of practically every variation his team will ever encounter. Below each illustration, if the situation warrants, is a reiteration of suggested combo calls.

On the fourth Figure of the set (Figure 3-6), are illustrated examples of backfield actions that could be used in conjunction with the master call. This page will show the reader how to adapt each master call to:

1. Split Backs
2. Weak Backs
3. Strong Backs
4. Toward the X End
5. A Slotback
6. A Wingback

One of the expressions that is frequently used in making comments about plays directed toward the X end is: "The play is only effective versus a reduced eight-man front." We use a twins formation to reduce an eight-man front. Figure 3-2, A and B shows two examples of how a split-4 defense would adjust to a twins formation. In Figure 3-2 A we see that the outside linebacker toward the two-receiver side of the offensive formation has walked away and is aligned opposite the slotback. We call this a "reduced eight-man front" because the defense has deviated from the normal alignment by reducing its front to only seven defenders. In Figure 3-2 B, however, the defense has not reduced its front to seven defenders. They are still playing a true eight-man front.

Figure 3-2

3-2A

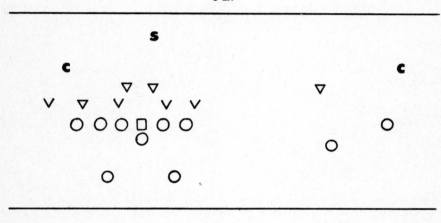

3-2B

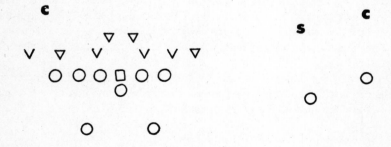

In formulating a strategy versus these two adjustments, a coach would obviously not want to direct running plays toward the X end versus defenses that did not reduce itself, because there are more defenders in this area than available blockers. On the other hand, running plays directed toward the X end are feasible versus a reduced front because the number of available blockers is equal to the number of defenders. When playing against teams that do not reduce their eight-man front, a coach would want to throw the ball. Nonreduced eight-man fronts must play man-to-man in the secondary, without the benefit of a free safety—and since the two twin receivers have the entire field to manipulate their defenders, the offense should be able to generate a very effective aerial attack. The balance of this chapter will present the playbook format used to teach Radar, Off-Tackle, Master Calls.

POWER

Comments and Coaching Points

1. This play develops more slowly than some other off-tackle schemes, but it insures maximum power at the point of attack.

2. The middle linebacker is not blocked versus the Pro 4-3, College 4-3, 4-3 Eagle or 6-5. The backside guard should watch him as he pulls and block him if he shoots one of the gaps. If this linebacker shuffles down the line, the guard should block him as he pulls through the hole. If the middle linebacker becomes a problem, discard this scheme and use Punch or Quick Y.

3. The frontside tight 6 linebacker is also not blocked. The backside guard should attempt to block him in the same manner as described above.

Figure 3-3

3-4   Split-4

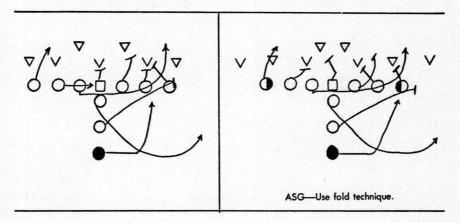

ASG—Use fold technique.

Figure 3-4

POSITIONS	RULE ASSIGNMENT			
ASE	EAGLE, INSIDE, LINEBACKER			
AST	RULE			
ASG	RULE (Use fold technique to block Split-4 inside linebacker)			
C	ON, AWAY			
BSG	PULL & LEAD			
BST	FILL			
BSE	DOWNFIELD			

POSITIONS	CROSSBLOCK	ZONE	POP	SCOOP
ASE & AST	5-3 Stack 6-5		5-3 Stack 6-5	
AST & ASG	Weak Gap Stack Eagle College 4-3 4-3 Eagle			
ASG & C				
C & BSG				
BSG & BST				
OTHER				

Figure 3-5

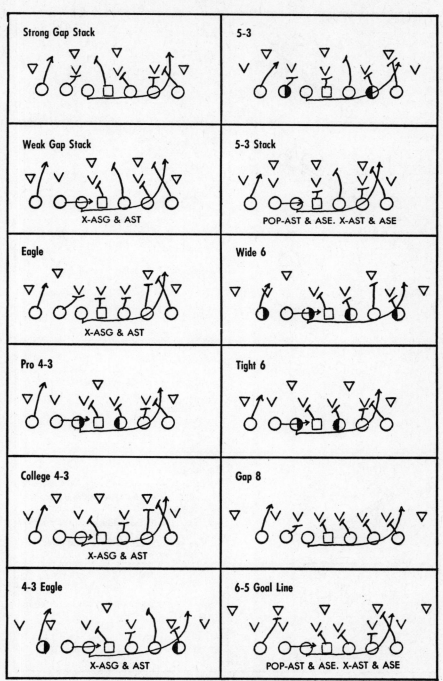

Figure 3-6

	Split Backs Good play.
	Weak Backs Good play.
	Strong Backs Good play. Fullback has to cheat back.
	Toward the X End 1. OK versus seven-man fronts. 2. Only good against an eight-man front if it is reduced.
	Slotback 1. Good play as diagrammed. Right halfback influences the defensive end & blocks the cornerback. 2. If run toward the slotback (not shown), the slotback blocks ASE rules. 3. Same backfield action as illustrated for Punch can also be used.
	Wingback Excellent—Wingback influences the defensive end.

PUNCH

Comments and Coaching Points

1. This is an extremely effective scheme versus stunting defenses. The success of the play is dependent upon the tight end's ability to block the defensive tackle one-on-one.

2. Punch, Squeeze, Stampede, Slant, Gut Trap and G Punch can all be combined to make up a devastating series.

3. The stack 5-3, tandem 5-3 Stack, and tandem 6-5 goal-line linebackers will be picked up by the pulling guard as he comes through the hole. If these players stunt, the offensive line will automatically be able to pick them up and block their stunt correctly. (How this will be accomplished will be covered in Chapter 7.)

Figure 3-7

3-4   Split-4

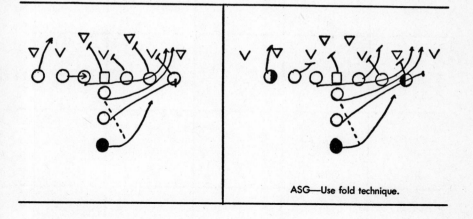

ASG—Use fold technique.

Figure 3-8

POSITIONS	RULE ALIGNMENT			
ASE	INSIDE, LINEBACKER			
AST	INSIDE, LINEBACKER			
ASG	INSIDE, LINEBACKER (Use fold technique to block Split-4 inside linebacker)			
C	AWAY			
BSG	PULL & LEAD			
BST	FILL			
BSE	DOWNFIELD			
POSITIONS	CROSSBLOCK	ZONE	POP	SCOOP
ASE & AST				
AST & ASG				
ASG & C				
C & BSG				
BSG & BST				
OTHER				

Figure 3-9

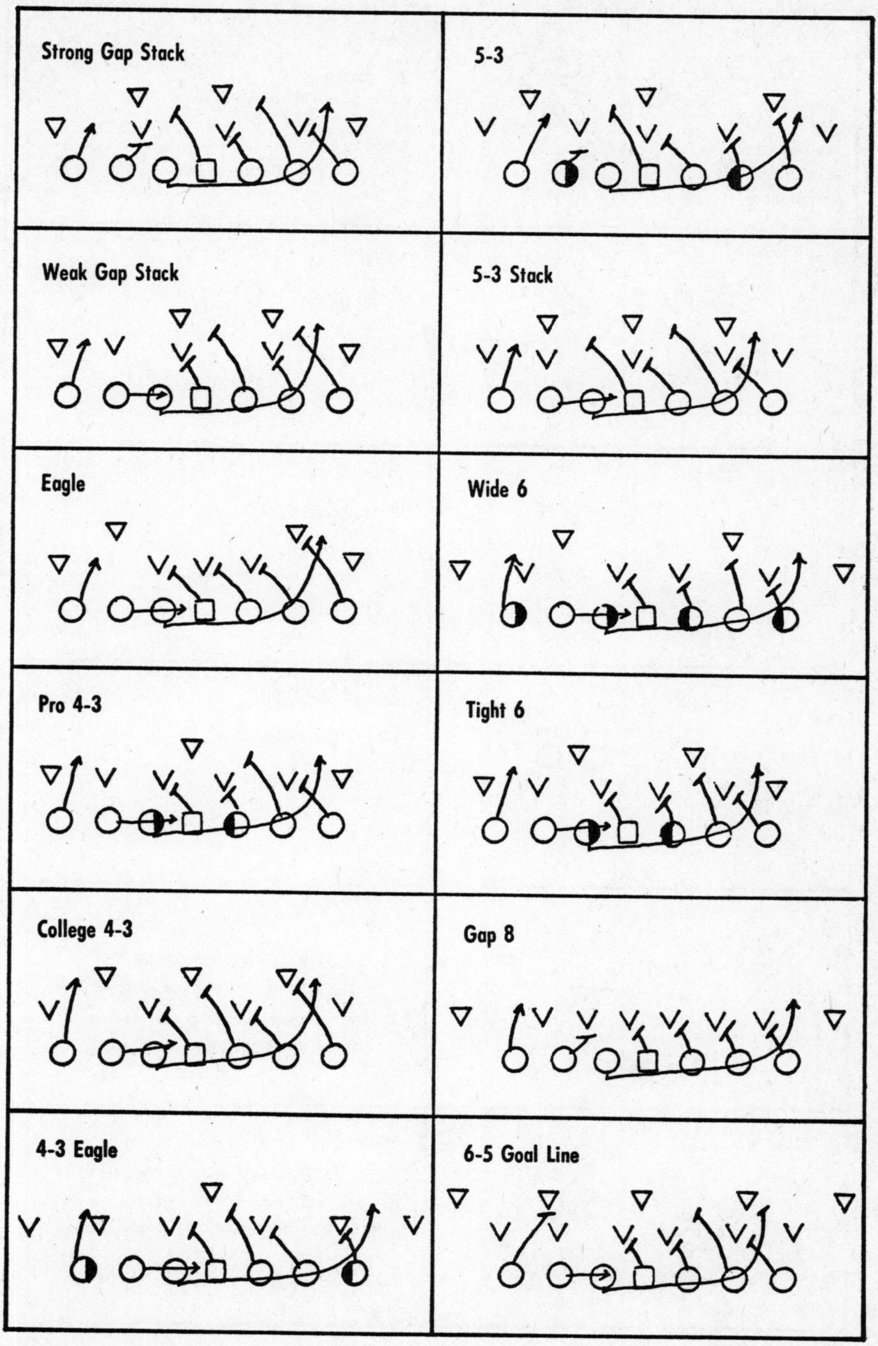
Strong Gap Stack
5-3
Weak Gap Stack
5-3 Stack
Eagle
Wide 6
Pro 4-3
Tight 6
College 4-3
Gap 8
4-3 Eagle
6-5 Goal Line

Figure 3-10

	Split Backs Excellent play.
	Weak Backs Good play.
	Strong Backs Not a good play.
	Toward the X End Not a good play.
	Slotback 1. The slotback can be sent into motion and used to block the end (as diagrammed). 2. The slotback can also be used as a ball carrier (see illustration for Power).
	Wingback Excellent. The wingback can be used to influence the end and block the cornerback, or he can be used to seal off a tandem linebacker.

G PUNCH

Comments and Coaching Points

1. This scheme should be used with counter-type plays.
2. Like the punch, it is extremely effective versus stunting defenses.
3. This scheme is very similar to Blast. Its advantage over Blast is that it does a better job of protecting the backside A Gap. The advantage that Blast has over G Punch is that Blast provides a lead blocker at the point of attack.

Figure 3-11

3-4   Split-4

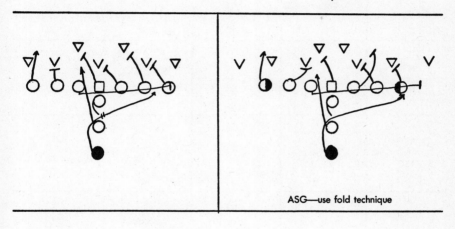

ASG—use fold technique

Figure 3-12

POSITIONS	RULE ASSIGNMENT			
ASE	INSIDE, LINEBACKER			
AST	TANDEM, INSIDE, LINEBACKER			
ASG	STACK, INSIDE, LINEBACKER (Split-4, use fold technique)			
C	ON VERSUS STACK OTHERWISE, AWAY			
BSG	PULL & TRAP			
BST	RULE			
BSE	DOWNFIELD			

POSITIONS	CROSSBLOCK	ZONE	POP	SCOOP
ASE & AST			5-3 Stack 6-5	
AST & ASG				
ASG & C			5-3 Stack 5-3	
C & BSG				
BSG & BST				
OTHER				

Figure 3-13

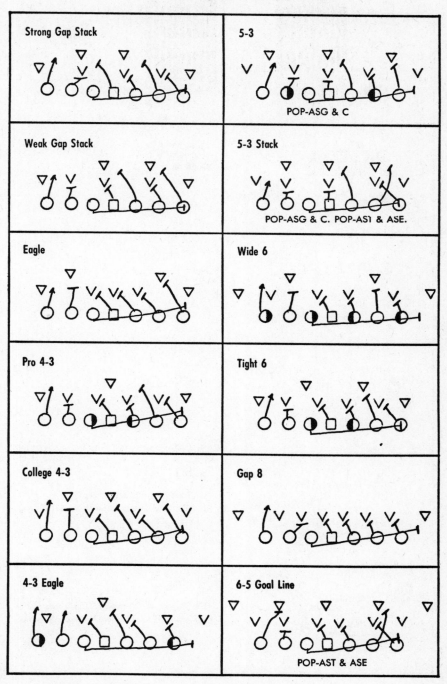

Figure 3-14

	Split Backs Good play.
	Weak Backs Good play.
	Strong Backs Not a good play.
	Toward the X End Not a good play.
	Slotback 1. Good play as diagrammed. 2. HB can be used to influence the end or lead through the hole.
	Wingback Great play as diagrammed. This is a double reverse with three backs leading through the hole.

BLAST

Comments and Coaching Points

1. Extremely effective if incorporated into a Wing-T type attack.
2. Any defender aligned in the backside A Gap is left unblocked by the offensive line. It is thus necessary to have the fullback fill this area against defenses that have a defender aligned in this gap.
3. If the tandem Linebacker is a 5-3 stack and the 6-5 goal-line linebacker is initially unblocked, the backside linebacker should block him as he pulls through the hole. If this defender stunts, the line will have no difficulty picking him up. (How this is accomplished will be covered in Chapter 7.)

Figure 3-15

3-4   Split-4

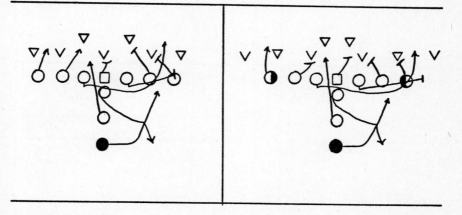

Figure 3-16

POSITIONS	RULE ASSIGNMENT
ASE	INSIDE, LINEBACKER
AST	INSIDE, LINEBACKER
ASG	PULL & TRAP
C	RULE
BSG	PULL & LEAD
BST	INSIDE, DOWNFIELD
BSE	DOWNFIELD

POSITIONS	CROSSBLOCK	ZONE	POP	SCOOP
ASE & AST				
AST & ASG				
ASG & C				
C & BSG				
BSG & BST				
OTHER		AST & C College 4-3 4-3 Eagle		

Figure 3-17

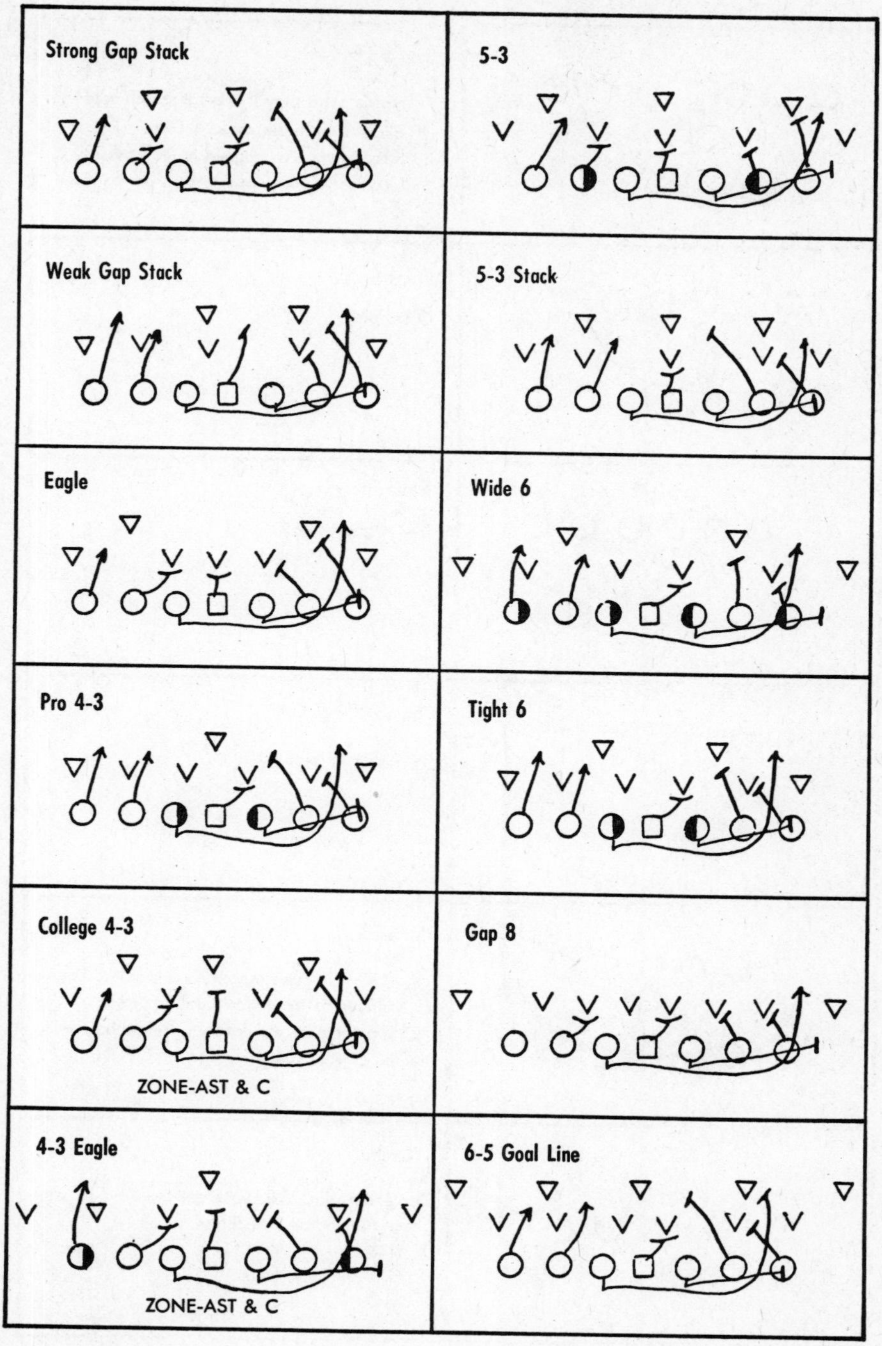

Strong Gap Stack	**5-3**
Weak Gap Stack	**5-3 Stack**
Eagle	**Wide 6**
Pro 4-3	**Tight 6**
College 4-3	**Gap 8**
ZONE-AST & C	
4-3 Eagle	**6-5 Goal Line**
ZONE-AST & C	

Figure 3-18

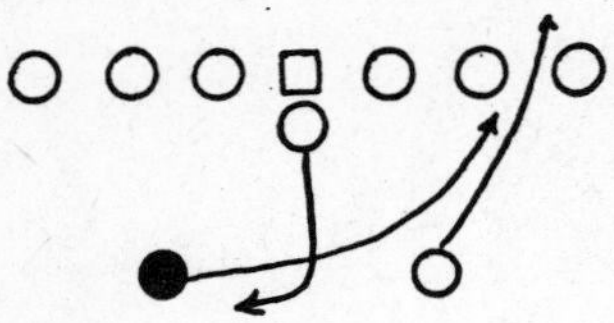	**Split Backs** 1. Not a good play if there is a defender aligned in the backside A Gap. 2. If no defender is aligned in the backside A Gap, the play could be run as diagrammed.
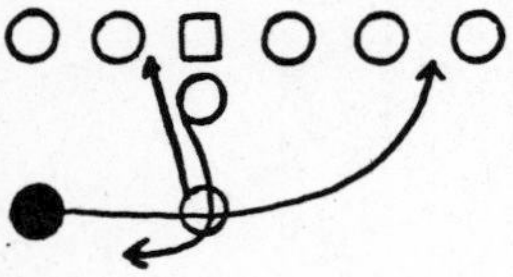	**Weak Backs** Good play.
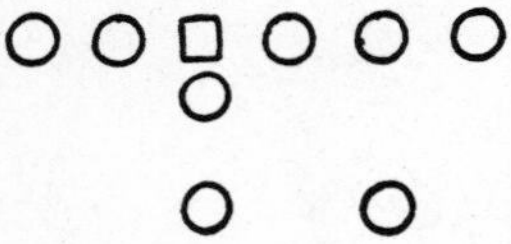	**Strong Backs** Not a good play.
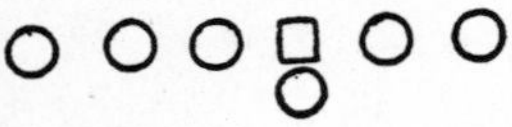	**Toward the X End** Not a good play.
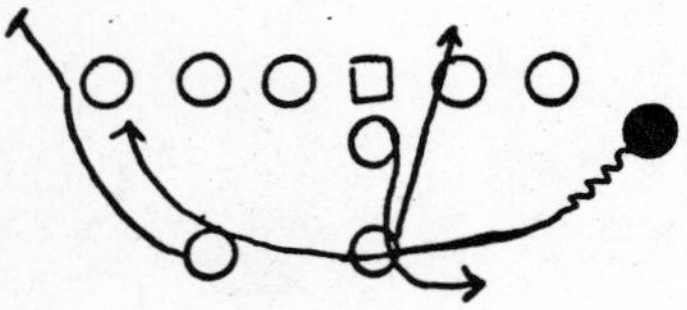	**Slotback** 1. Good play as diagrammed, right halfback influences the end and blocks the corner. 2. If run toward the slotback, the slotback will block ASE rules.
	**Wingback** Excellent play. Wingback can be used to influence the end and block the corner.

QUICK

Comments and Coaching Points

1. Good scheme to engineer quick-hitting off-tackle plays. It is extremely effective versus defenses that like to play off the line in an attempt to stop sweeps and traps.

2. If Quick is used to run the option, the attackside end's rule should be changed to: EAGLE, DOWNFIELD.

3. A lead back must block the defensive end versus every eight-man front except the tight-6.

Figure 3-19

3-4	Split-4

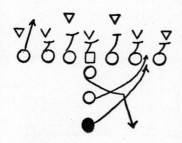 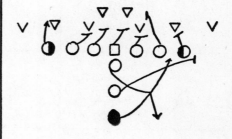

| X-BSG & BST, SCOOP, ZONE-ASG & AST | X-AST & ASG, POP-ASG & AST |

Figure 3-20

POSITIONS	RULE ASSIGNMENT			
ASE	EAGLE, OUTSIDE			
AST	ON, OVER, LINEBACKER			
ASG	ON, OVER, REACH, LINEBACKER			
C	RULE			
BSG	RULE			
BST	RULE			
BSE	DOWNFIELD			

POSITIONS	CROSSBLOCK	ZONE	POP	SCOOP
ASE & AST	3-4 Strong Gap Stack Pro 4-3 College 4-3 5-3 Stack Tight 6 6-5		5-3 Stack 6-5	
AST & ASG	Split-4 Weak Gap Stack Eagle College 4-3 4-3 Eagle	3-4	Split-4	
ASG & C		Pro 4-3 College 4-3	5-3 5-3 Stack	
C & BSG	Weak Gap Stack College 4-3 4-3 Eagle			3-4
BSG & BST	3-4 Strong Gap Stack 5-3 5-3 Stack			
OTHER				

Figure 3-21

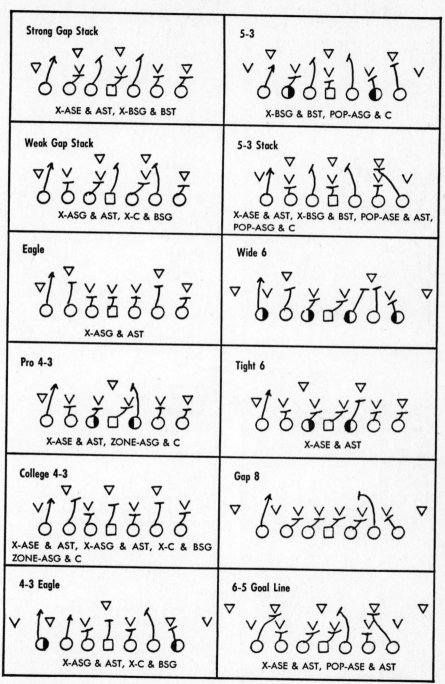

Strong Gap Stack
X-ASE & AST, X-BSG & BST

Weak Gap Stack
X-ASG & AST, X-C & BSG

Eagle
X-ASG & AST

Pro 4-3
X-ASE & AST, ZONE-ASG & C

College 4-3
X-ASE & AST, X-ASG & AST, X-C & BSG
ZONE-ASG & C

4-3 Eagle
X-ASG & AST, X-C & BSG

5-3
X-BSG & BST, POP-ASG & C

5-3 Stack
X-ASE & AST, X-BSG & BST, POP-ASE & AST,
POP-ASG & C

Wide 6

Tight 6
X-ASE & AST

Gap 8

6-5 Goal Line
X-ASE & AST, POP-ASE & AST

Figure 3-22

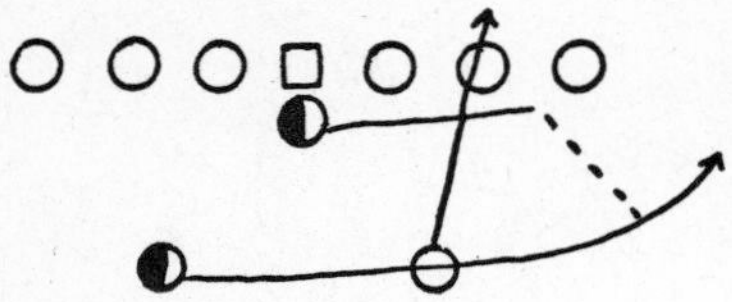

Split Backs

1. Good dive option rules.
2. If used for this purpose, change the ASE's rules to: EAGLE, DOWNFIELD.

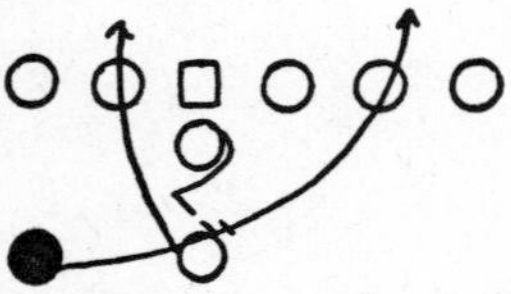

Weak Backs

1. Good versus defenses in which no lead is necessary.
2. Could also give the ball to the halfback and have the fullback lead.

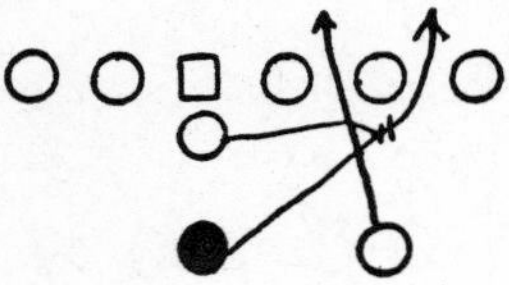

Strong Backs

Good play.

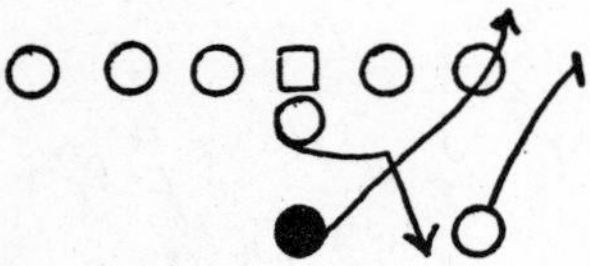

Toward the X End

Good versus: 3-4, Weak Gap Stack, Strong Gap Stack, Eagle, Pro 4-3, College 4-3, 4-3 Eagle or any eight-man front that has been reduced.

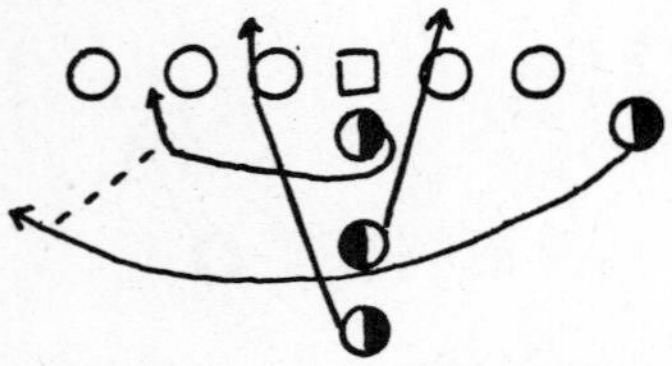

Slotback

1. Good double dive-option series.
2. If used for this purpose, change the ASE's rules to EAGLE, DOWNFIELD.

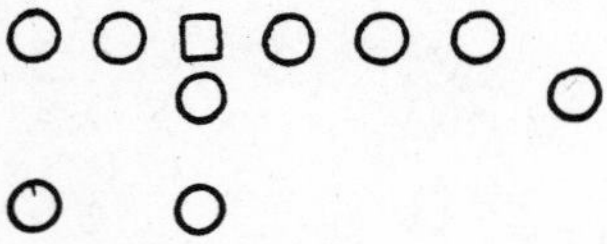

Wingback

1. Good play toward the wingback. The wing can be used as a lead blocker or he can influence the end.
2. Good away from the wingback (if a lead back is used) versus any seven-man front.

QUICK Y

Comments and Coaching Points

1. Like Quick, this scheme should be used with quick-hitting off-tackle plays.
2. All defenders are blocked. This scheme is sound versus all defenses and should be used when stunting defenses are penetrating the power (Punch can also be used in this situation).
3. The Quick Y scheme can also be used with the outside veer or speed option.

Figure 3-23

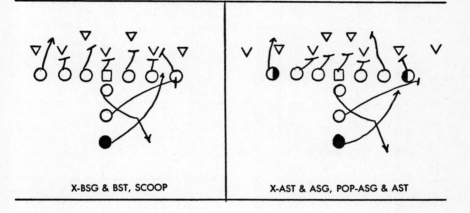

3-4	Split-4
X-BSG & BST, SCOOP	X-AST & ASG, POP-ASG & AST

Figure 3-24

POSITIONS	RULE ASSIGNMENT
ASE	EAGLE, INSIDE, LINEBACKER
AST	ON, OVER, LINEBACKER
ASG	ON, OVER, REACH, LINEBACKER
C	RULE
BSG	RULE
BST	RULE
BSE	DOWNFIELD

POSITIONS	CROSSBLOCK	ZONE	POP	SCOOP
ASE & AST	5-3 Stack 6-5		5-3 Stack 6-5	
AST & ASG	Split-4 Weak Gap Stack Eagle College 4-3 4-3 Eagle		Split-4	
ASG & C		Pro 4-3 College 4-3	5-3 5-3 Stack	
C & BSG	Weak Gap Stack College 4-3 4-3 Eagle			3-4
BSG & BST	3-4 Strong Gap Stack 5-3 5-3 Stack			
OTHER				

Figure 3-25

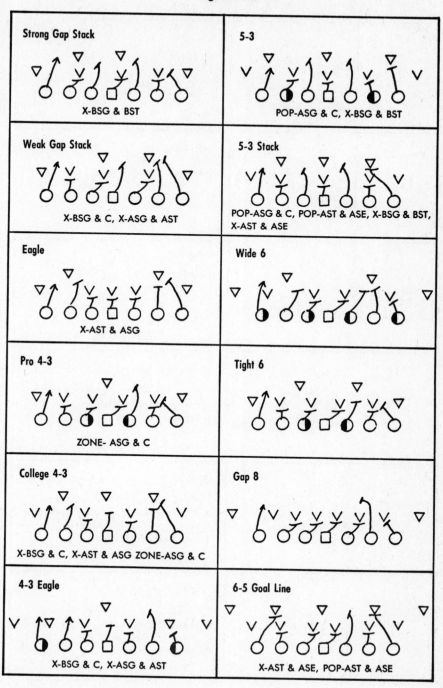

Figure 3-26

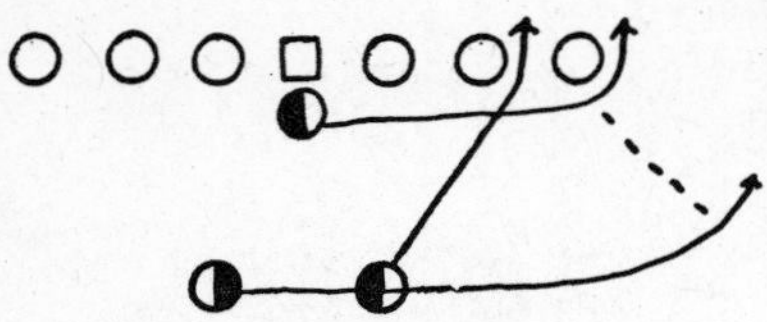

Split Backs

Good scheme for the outside veer.

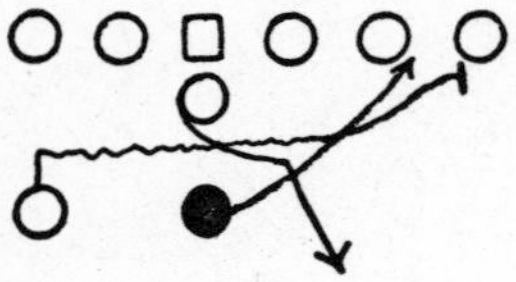

Weak Backs

Good play.

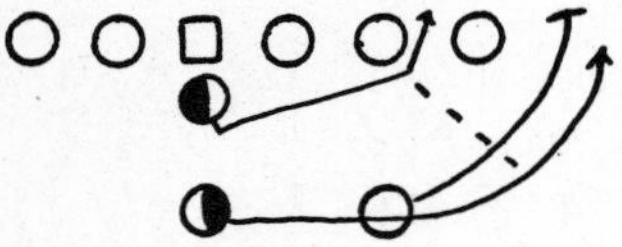

Strong Backs

Good scheme for the speed option.

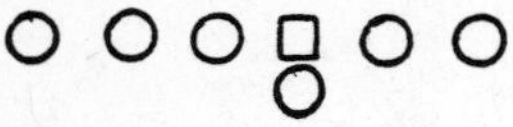

Toward the X End

1. Good play versus any seven-man front or any reduced eight-man front.
2. Any backfield set is OK.

Slotback

1. Good play to or away from the slot.
2. If toward the slot, slotback blocks ASE rules.
3. Any backfield set is OK.

Wingback

1. Good toward or away from the wing.
2. If toward the wing, wingback can influence the end or lead through the hole.
3. Any backfield set is OK.

SLANT

Comments and Coaching Points

1. The play is a quick thrust, characterized by angle blocking and the trapping of the defensive end.

2. This is an extremely effective scheme versus hard charging, penetrating defenses.

3. A lead block by an offensive back is needed versus: Split-4 Inside LB, 5-3 Middle LB, 5-3 Stack and 6-5 Tandem linebackers.

Figure 3-27

3-4   Split-4

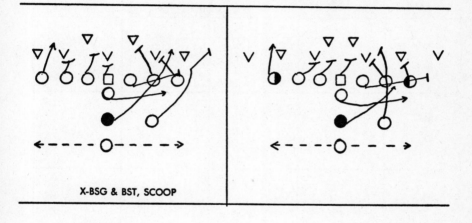

X-BSG & BST, SCOOP

Figure 3-28

POSITIONS	RULE ASSIGNMENT			
ASE	INSIDE, LINEBACKER			
AST	INSIDE, LINEBACKER			
ASG	PULL & TRAP			
C	RULE			
BSG	RULE			
BST	RULE			
BSE	DOWNFIELD			

POSITIONS	CROSSBLOCK	ZONE	POP	SCOOP
ASE & AST				
AST & ASG				
ASG & C				
C & BSG	Weak Gap Stack College 4-3 4-3 Eagle			3-4 5-3
BSG & BST	3-4 Strong Gap Stack 5-3 5-3 Stack			
OTHER		AST & C College 4-3 4-3 Eagle		

Figure 3-29

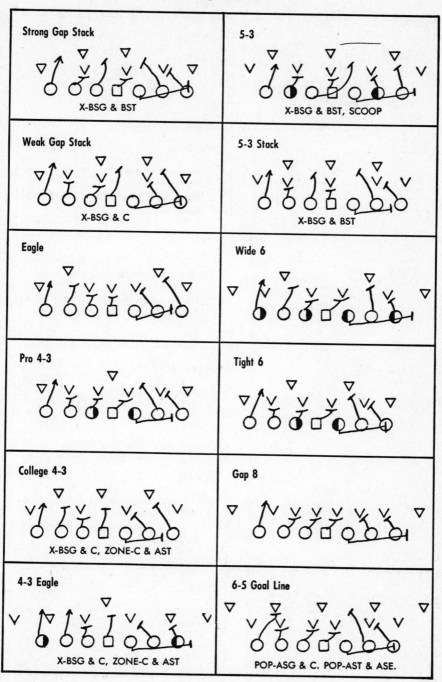

Figure 3-30

	Split Backs Good play.
	Weak Backs 1. Good versus every defense in which a lead is not needed. 2. Good play to be used in conjunction with the outside veer.
	Strong Backs 1. QB first fakes to the HB and then gives to the FB. 2. The HB can also be used to lead through the hole or influence the defensive end.
	Toward the X End Not a good play.
	Slotback 1. If toward the slotback, the slotback blocks the ASE rules. 2. Good toward the tight end with any backfield set.
	Wingback Wingback can be used to influence the end or as a lead blocker.

BEND

Comments and Coaching Points

1. Good scheme versus reading defenses, but it is poor versus stunting, penetrating defenses.
2. Bend should be used with quick-hitting off-tackle plays. No lead back is necessary.

Figure 3-31

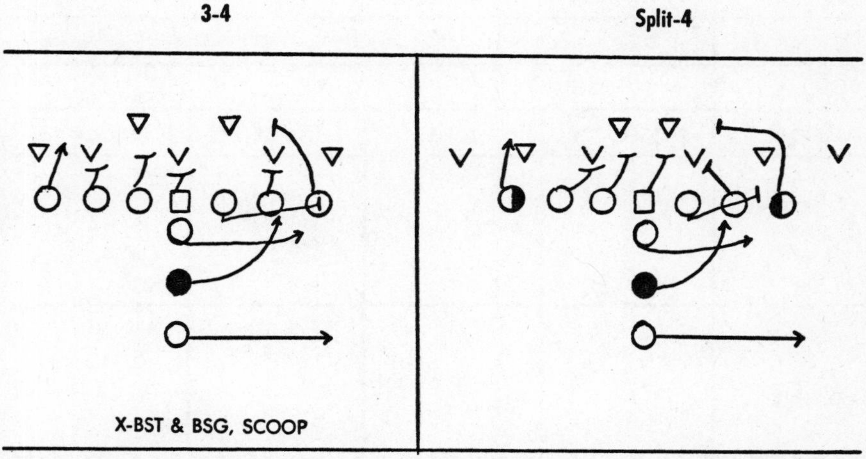

3-4   Split-4

X-BST & BSG, SCOOP

Figure 3-32

POSITIONS	RULE ASSIGNMENT
ASE	LINEBACKER
AST	INSIDE, ON, OVER, LINEBACKER
ASG	PULL & TRAP
C	RULE
BSG	STACK, RULE
BST	RULE
BSE	DOWNFIELD

POSITIONS	CROSSBLOCK	ZONE	POP	SCOOP
ASE & AST			5-3 Stack 6-5	
AST & ASG				
ASG & C				
C & BSG	Weak Gap Stack College 4-3 4-3 Eagle			5-3 5-3 Stack 3-4
BSG & BST	Strong Gap Stack 3-4			
OTHER				

Figure 3-33

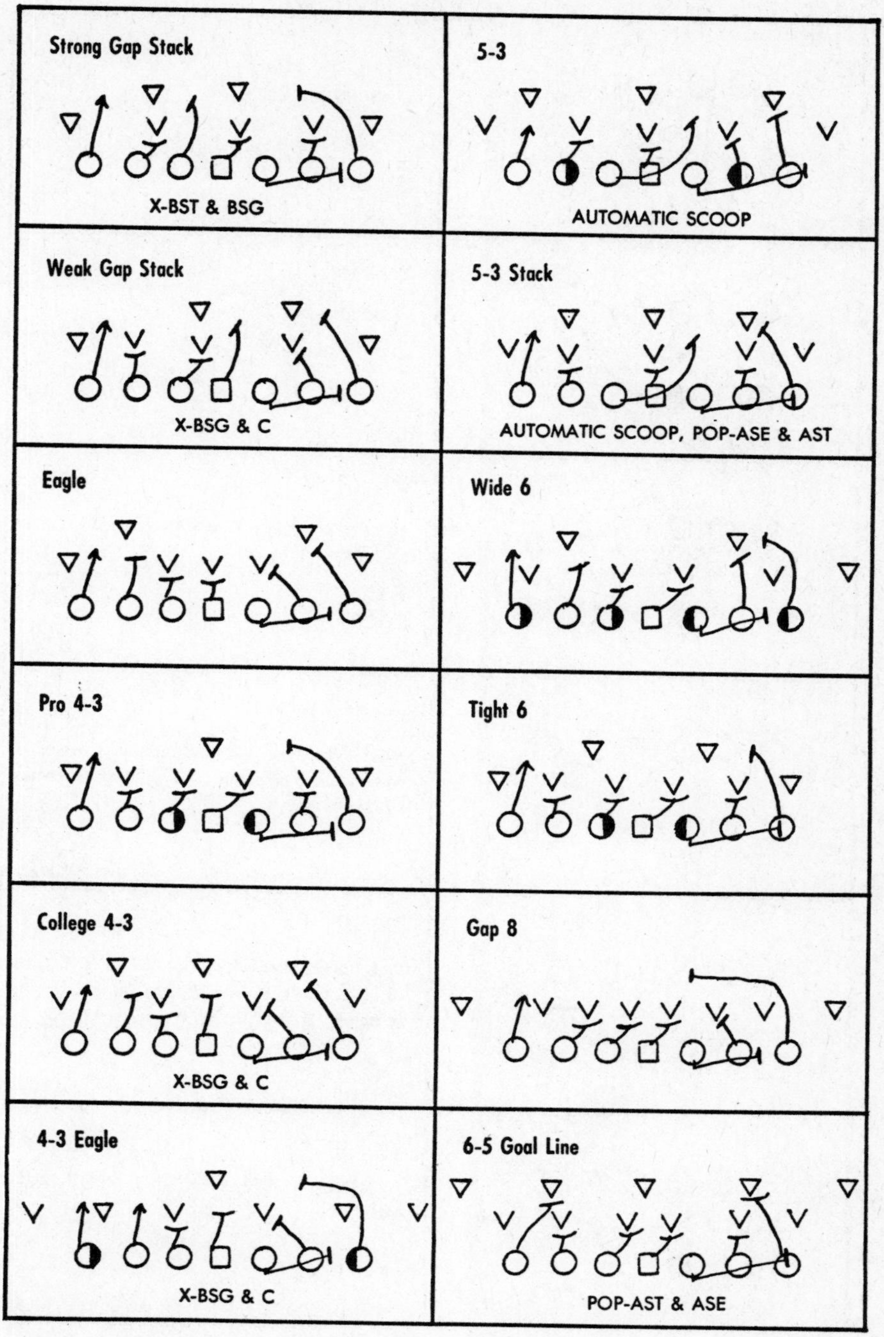

Strong Gap Stack — X-BST & BSG	**5-3** — AUTOMATIC SCOOP
Weak Gap Stack — X-BSG & C	**5-3 Stack** — AUTOMATIC SCOOP, POP-ASE & AST
Eagle	**Wide 6**
Pro 4-3	**Tight 6**
College 4-3 — X-BSG & C	**Gap 8**
4-3 Eagle — X-BSG & C	**6-5 Goal Line** — POP-AST & ASE

Figure 3-34

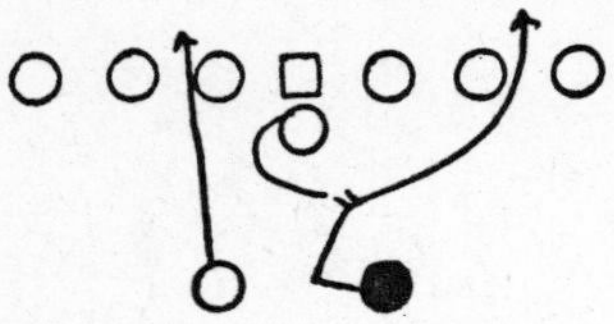	**Split Backs** Good play.
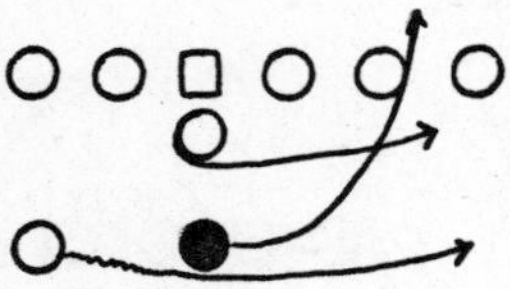	**Weak Backs** Good play.
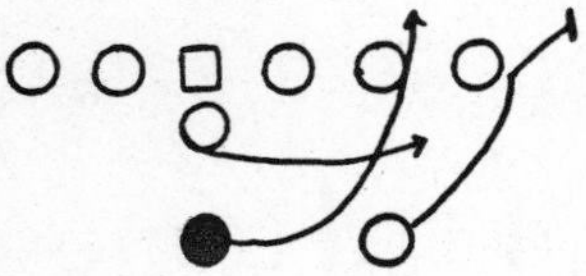	**Strong Backs** Good play. HB can influence the defensive end or lead through the hole.
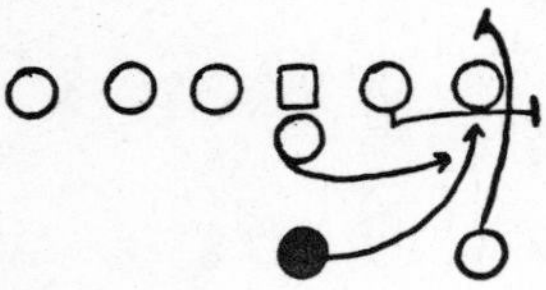	**Toward the X End** HB blocks ASE rules. Good play versus all seven-man fronts and all reduced eight-man fronts.
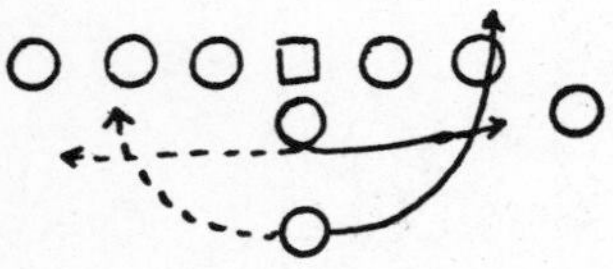	**Slotback** Good play. Slotback blocks ASE rules. Because of his depth it is easier for the SB to block the scrapping Split-4 LB than it is the tight end.
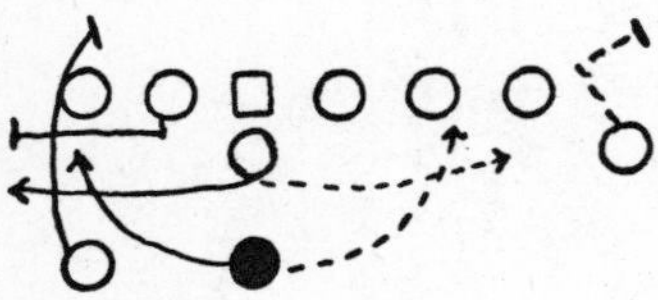	**Wingback** Good play. Wingback can influence the defensive end.

SLICE

Comments and Coaching Points

1. Slice is a variation of Bend.
2. Versus a Strong Gap Stack, Pro 4-3, Tight 6, and 6-5, a lead back is needed to block the attackside linebacker.
3. The difference between Bend and Slice is that Slice attempts to double-team a defender playing On the offensive tackle whenever feasible.

Figure 3-35

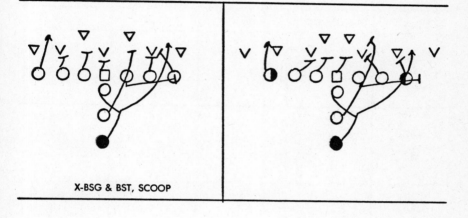

3-4 Split-4

X-BSG & BST, SCOOP

Figure 3-36

POSITIONS	RULE ASSIGNMENT
ASE	EAGLE, INSIDE, LINEBACKER
AST	INSIDE, ON, OVER, LINEBACKER
ASG	PULL & TRAP
C	RULE
BSG	STACK, RULE
BST	RULE
BSE	DOWNFIELD

POSITIONS	CROSSBLOCK	ZONE	POP	SCOOP
ASE & AST			5-3 Stack 6-5	
AST & ASG				
ASG & C				
C & BSG	Weak Gap Stack College 4-3 4-3 Eagle			5-3 5-3 Stack 3-4
BSG & BST	Strong Gap Stack 3-4			
OTHER				

Figure 3-37

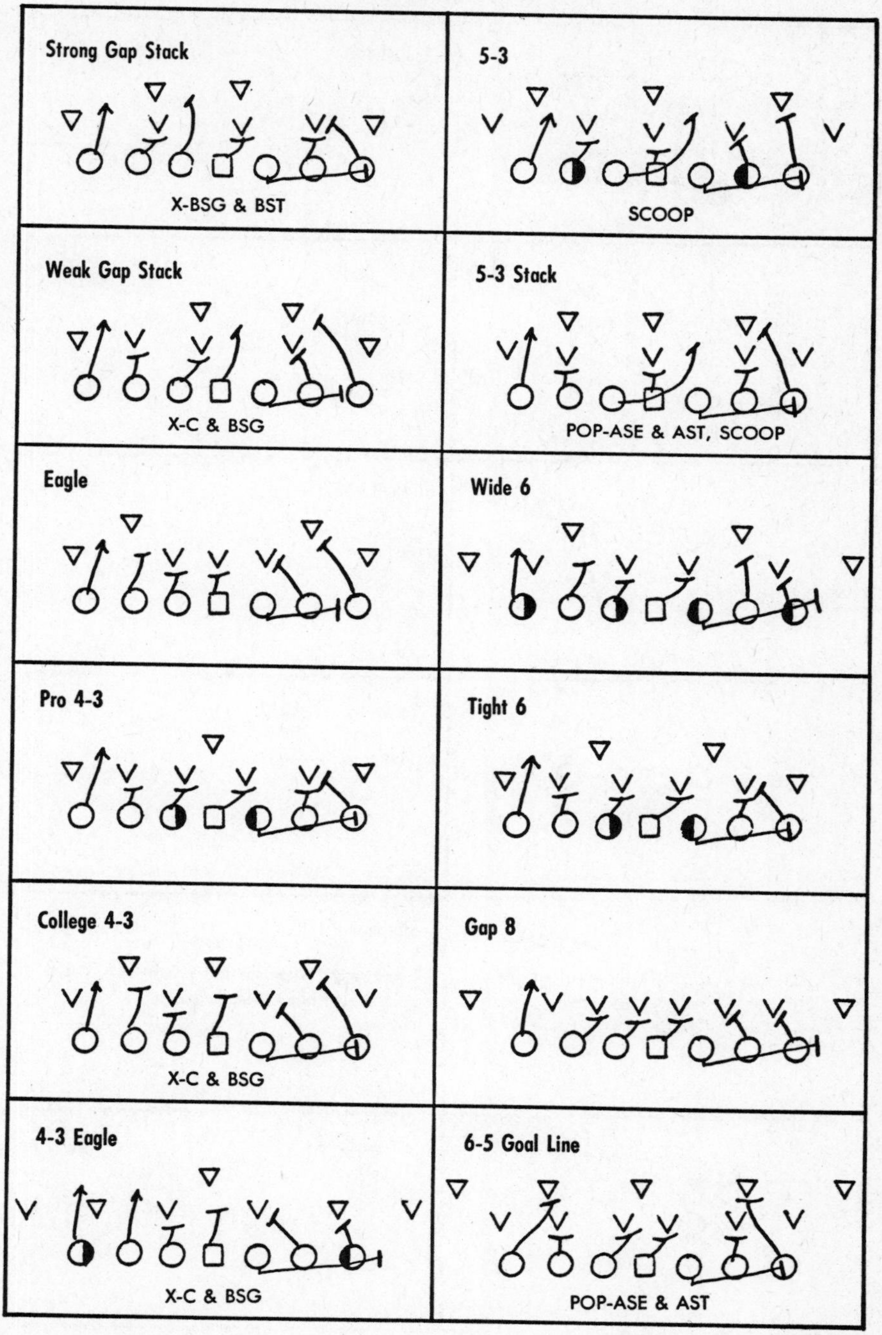

Strong Gap Stack	**5-3**
X-BSG & BST	SCOOP
Weak Gap Stack	**5-3 Stack**
X-C & BSG	POP-ASE & AST, SCOOP
Eagle	**Wide 6**
Pro 4-3	**Tight 6**
College 4-3	**Gap 8**
X-C & BSG	
4-3 Eagle	**6-5 Goal Line**
X-C & BSG	POP-ASE & AST

Figure 3-38

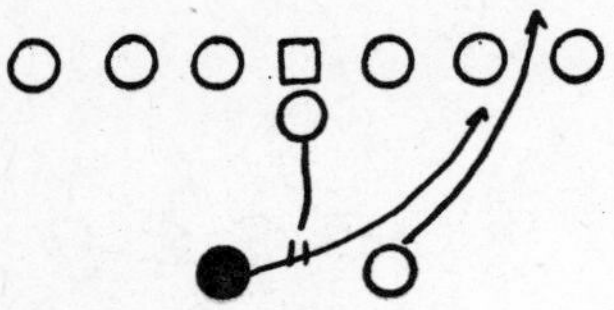	**Split Backs** OK.
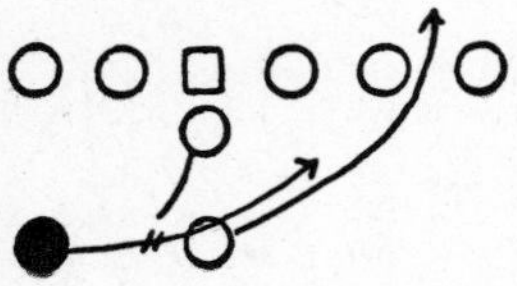	**Weak Backs** Fair play.
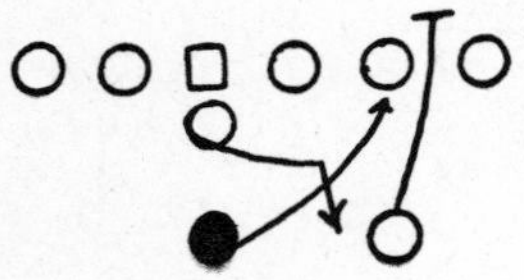	**Strong Backs** Excellent play.
	**Toward the X End** Not a good play.
	**Slotback** Good play. When run toward the slot, the slotback should block ASE rules.
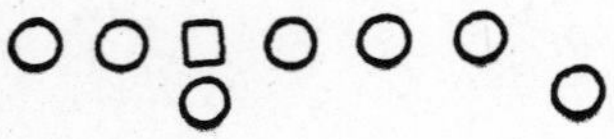	**Wingback** OK.

RIP

Comments and Coaching Points

1. Rip is another variation of Bend.

2. Unlike Bend and Slice, a lead back is always needed to block the attackside linebacker.

3. Rip is a good play versus the 3-4, Split-4, Weak Gap Stack, Eagle, College 4-3, 5-3 and 5-3 Stack. It is only fair or poor versus other defenses.

4. The difference between Rip and Bend is that the attackside end releases downfield whenever he is not confronted by a defender playing outside of him.

Figure 3-39

3-4   Split-4

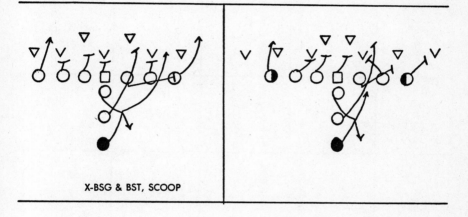

X-BSG & BST, SCOOP

Figure 3-40

POSITIONS	RULE ASSIGNMENT			
ASE	OUTSIDE, DOWNFIELD			
AST	ON, INSIDE			
ASG	PULL & TRAP			
C	RULE			
BSG	STACK, RULE			
BST	RULE			
BSE	DOWNFIELD			

POSITIONS	CROSSBLOCK	ZONE	POP	SCOOP
ASE & AST				
AST & ASG				
ASG & C				
C & BSG	Weak Gap Stack College 4-3 4-3 Eagle			5-3 5-3 Stack 3-4
BSG & BST	Strong Gap Stack 3-4			
OTHER				

Figure 3-41

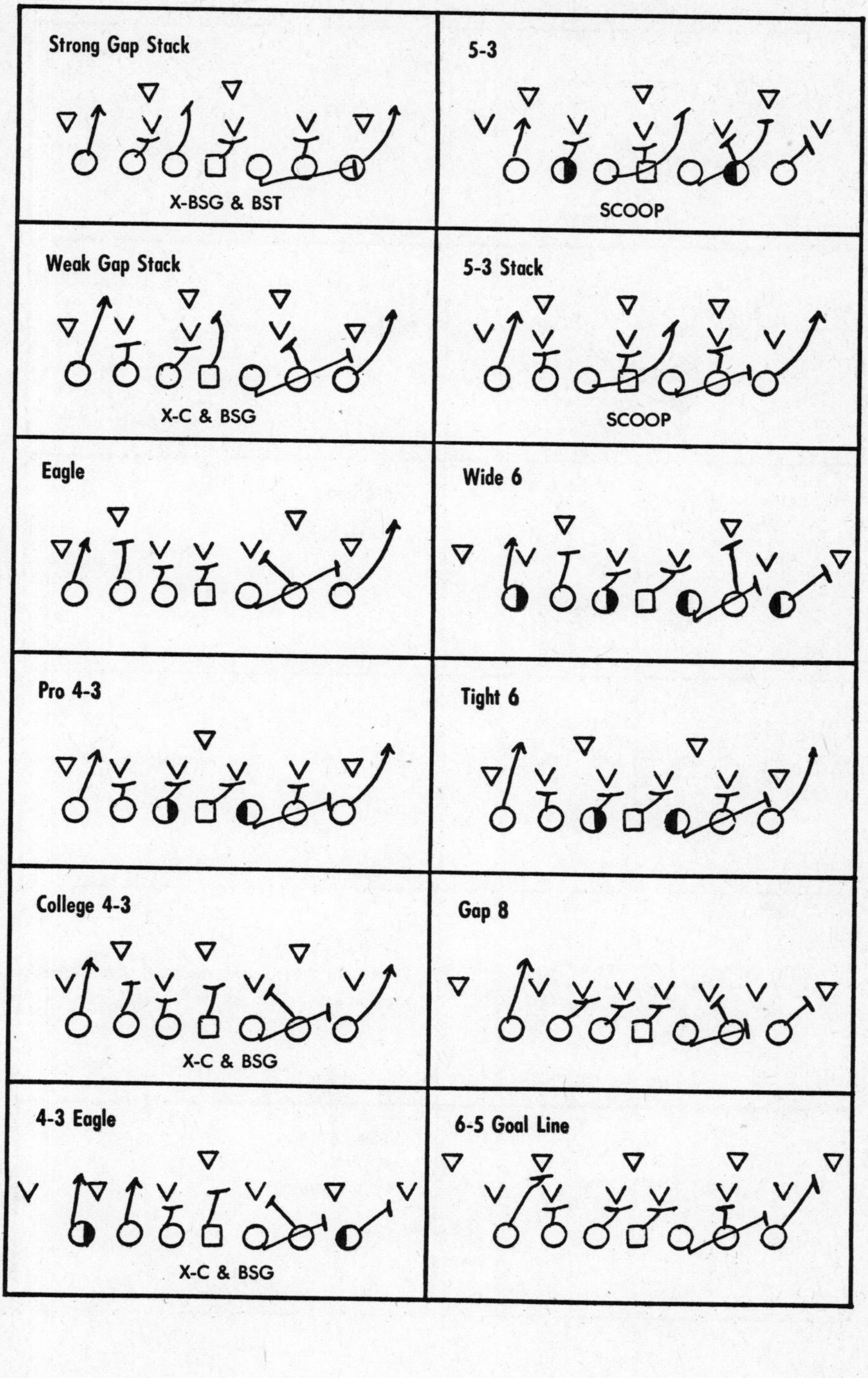

Strong Gap Stack	**5-3**
X-BSG & BST	SCOOP
Weak Gap Stack	**5-3 Stack**
X-C & BSG	SCOOP
Eagle	**Wide 6**
Pro 4-3	**Tight 6**
College 4-3	**Gap 8**
X-C & BSG	
4-3 Eagle	**6-5 Goal Line**
X-C & BSG	

Figure 3-42

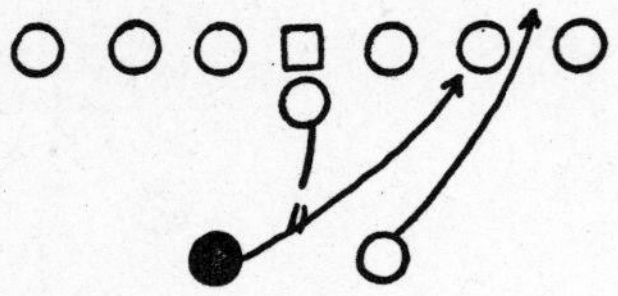	**Split Backs** Good play.
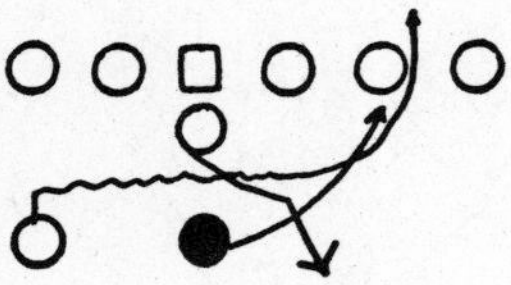	**Weak Backs** Fair play.
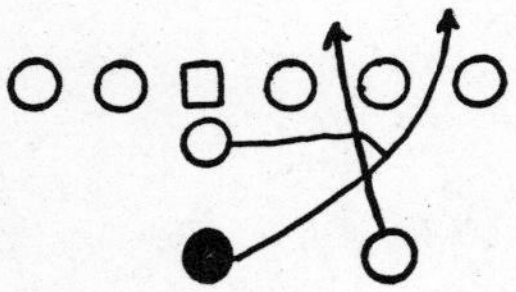	**Strong Backs** Excellent play.
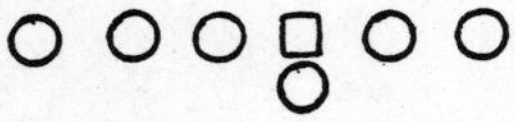	**Toward the X End** Good play against defenses noted on Figure 3-39
	**Slotback** Good play. If toward the slot, the slotback should block ASE rules.
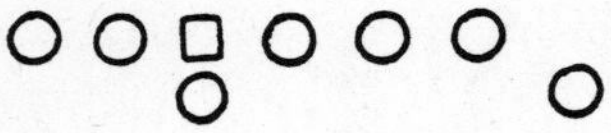	**Wingback** Not a good play.

TRAP OPTION

Comments and Coaching Points

1. Versus the 4-3 Eagle, Split-4, 5-3, Wide-6 and Gap 8, the Trap Option is much more effective toward the split end side.
2. The Trap Option is fantastic versus a reduced eight-man front.
3. Although the Trap Option is the only scheme labeled "option," Quick Y can be used for the speed option and the outside veer. Quick can be used for the dive option and veer can be used for the triple option.

Figure 3-43

3-4   Split-4

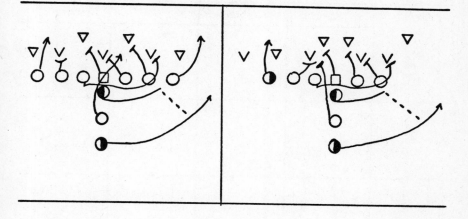

Figure 3-44

POSITIONS	RULE ASSIGNMENT			
ASE	DOWNFIELD			
AST	TANDEM, INSIDE, LINEBACKER			
ASG	STACK, INSIDE, LINEBACKER			
C	IF STACK BLOCK ON, OTHERWISE BLOCK AWAY			
BSG	PULL & OVERBLOCK THE FIRST DEFENDER OUTSIDE OF THE TACKLE'S BLOCK			
BST	RULE			
BSE	DOWNFIELD			

POSITIONS	CROSSBLOCK	ZONE	POP	SCOOP
ASE & AST				
AST & ASG				
ASG & C				
C & BSG				
BSG & BST				
OTHER				

Figure 3-45

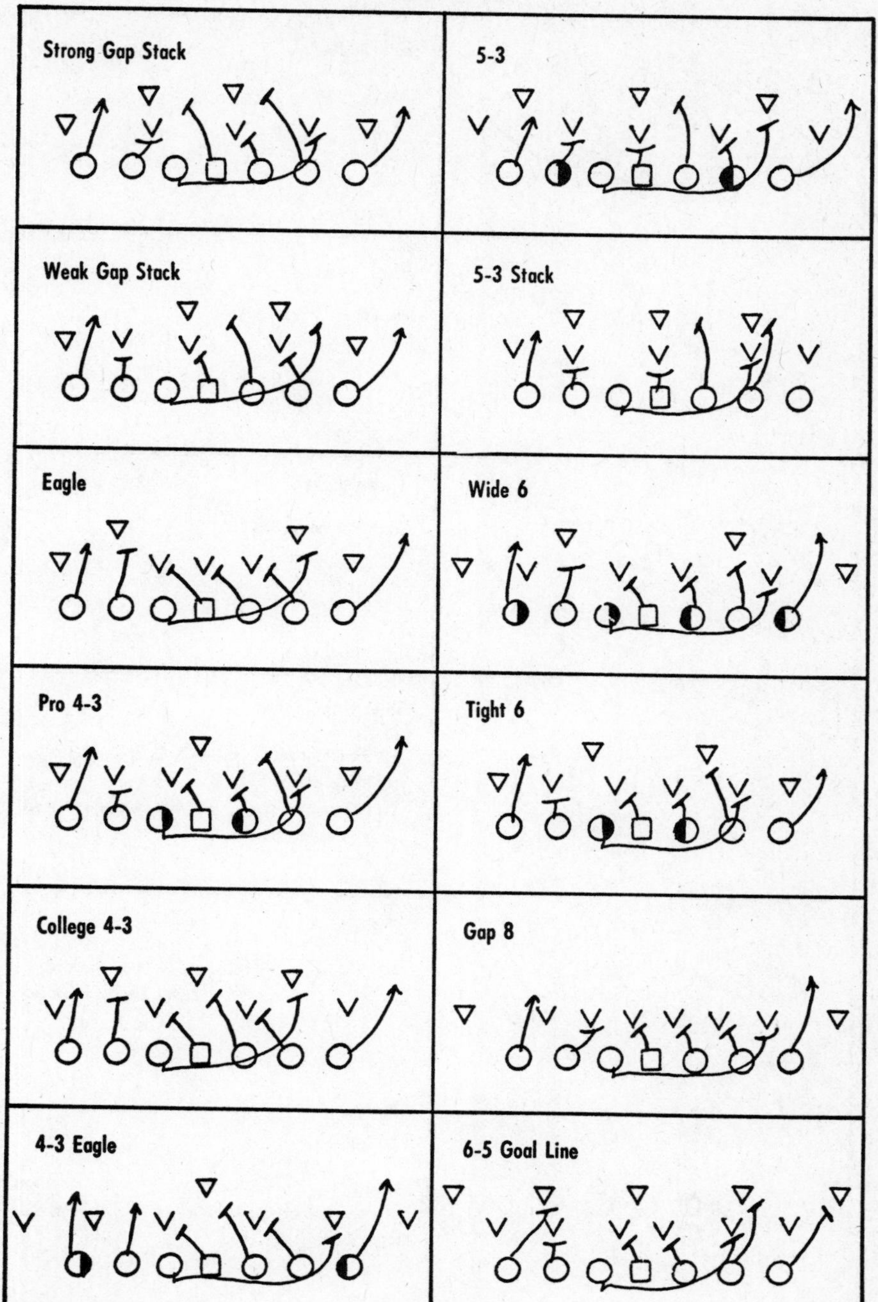

Strong Gap Stack	**5-3**
Weak Gap Stack	**5-3 Stack**
Eagle	**Wide 6**
Pro 4-3	**Tight 6**
College 4-3	**Gap 8**
4-3 Eagle	**6-5 Goal Line**

Figure 3-46

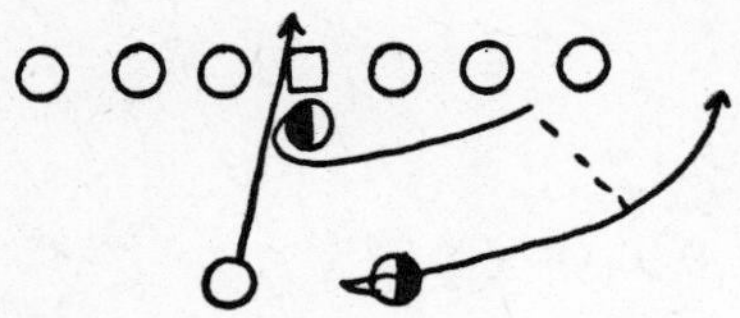

	Split Backs Excellent play.
	**Weak Backs** Excellent Wing-T play.
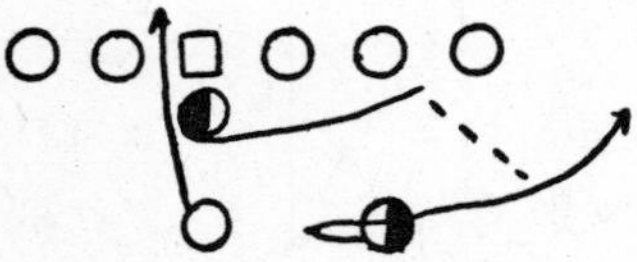	**Strong Backs** Excellent play.
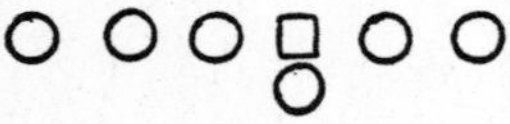	**Toward the X End** 1. Excellent versus the 4-3, Split-4, 5-3, Wide-6 and Gap 8. 2. Fantastic toward a twin versus reduced eight-man front.
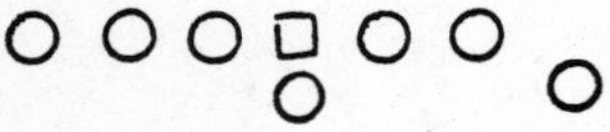	**Slotback** 1. Excellent play to or away from the slot. 2. When toward the slot, the slotback blocks ASE rules.
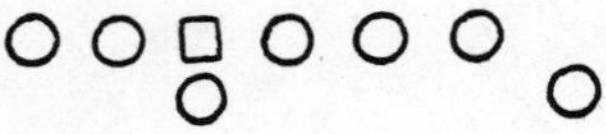	**Wingback** Good play if used in conjunction with the Wing-T offense. Otherwise it is better to spread the defense out.

Seal and Reach

We have faced a number of opponents who have attempted to stop our running game by getting into stack defenses and simply stunting defenders into every gap. Figure 3-47 illustrates the two most common defenses that we have encountered employing this tactic.

Figure 3-47

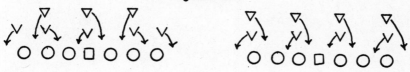

Since we have integrated combo calls into our system, we no longer experience difficulty dealing with this problem. We simply "Scoop" or "Pop" the stack, depending upon which sector we are attempting to attack. Seal and Reach have thus become obsolete master calls for us. Teams that are unable to incorporate combo calls into their system (*example*—lower division teams at the high school level) will find they experience difficulty versus the stack-stunt tactic. Seal and Reach is the solution to their problem.

Seal should be used with off-tackle plays that take longer to develop and Reach should be used with quick-hitting plays. The assignments for Seal and Reach are as follows:

Seal

ASE—Block C Gap

AST—Block B Gap

ASG—Block A Gap

C—Block Backside A Gap

BSG—Pull and Lead

BST—Block B Gap

BSE—Downfield

Reach

ASE—Block D Gap

AST—Block C Gap

ASG—Block B Gap

C—Block Frontside A Gap

BSG—Block A Gap

BST—Block B Gap

BSE—Downfield

Figure 3-48 illustrates Seal and Figure 3-49 illustrates Reach.

Figure 3-48

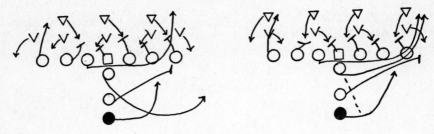

Figure 3-49

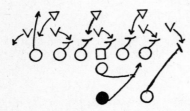

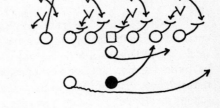

Reach can be used with quick-hitting plays directed toward the X end if a lead back blocks the end.

4

Attacking the Inside Sector of Modern Defenses

QUICK

Comments and Coaching Points

1. Quick is the base scheme. Its rules are effective versus all defensive sets. It is most successful against defenses that play off the line to stop the traps and sweeps.

2. If a coach preferred to have the tight end release downfield, rather than block the defensive end (a much more desirable scheme for the dive option play), he should change the ASE's rule to: EAGLE, DOWNFIELD.

3. A crossblock between the center and attackside guard versus the 4-3 Eagle and College 4-3 creates a new scheme. A crossblock between the attackside tackle and the attackside guard versus the 3-4 and college 4-3 creates still another scheme.

Figure 4-1

3-4

Split-4

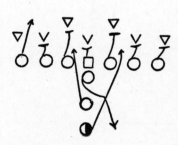

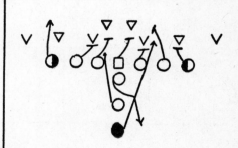

X:AST & ASG, X:BSG & BST, ZONE: ASG & AST, SCOOP

X:AST & ASG, POP:AST & ASG

Figure 4-2

POSITIONS	RULE ASSIGNMENT			
ASE	EAGLE, OVER, OUTSIDE			
AST	ON, OVER, LINEBACKER			
ASG	ON, OVER, REACH, LINEBACKER			
C	RULE			
BSG	RULE			
BST	RULE			
BSE	DOWNFIELD			
POSITIONS	CROSSBLOCK	ZONE	POP	SCOOP
ASE & AST				
AST & ASG	Split-4 Weak Gap Stack Eagle College 4-3 4-3 Eagle 3-4	3-4	Split-4	
ASG & C	4-3 Eagle College 4-3	Pro 4-3 College 4-3	5-3 5-3 Stack	
C & BSG	Weak Gap Stack College 4-3 4-3 Eagle			3-4
BSG & BST	3-4 Strong Gap Stack 5-3 5-3 Stack			
OTHER				

Figure 4-3

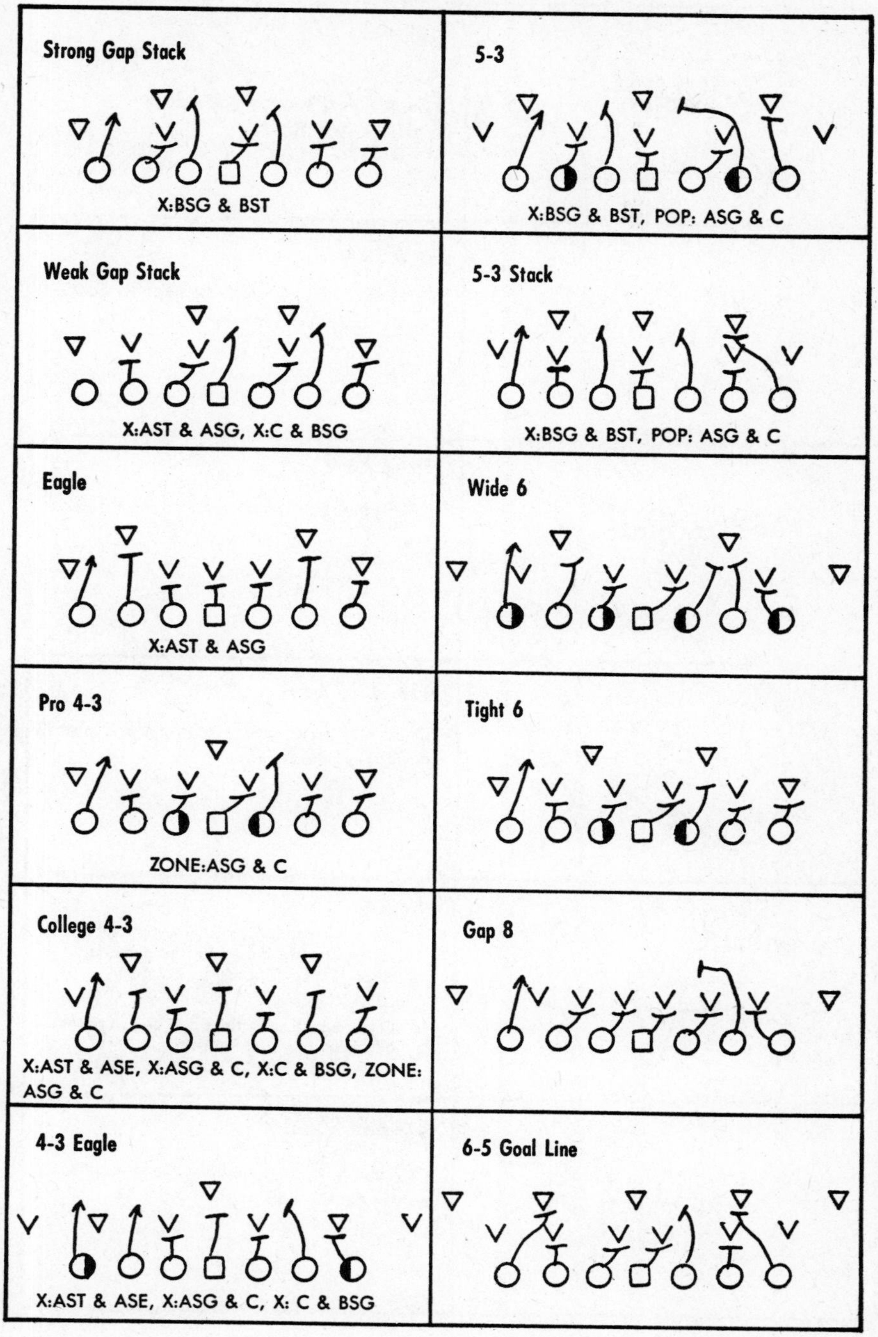

Strong Gap Stack X:BSG & BST	**5-3** X:BSG & BST, POP: ASG & C
Weak Gap Stack X:AST & ASG, X:C & BSG	**5-3 Stack** X:BSG & BST, POP: ASG & C
Eagle X:AST & ASG	**Wide 6**
Pro 4-3 ZONE:ASG & C	**Tight 6**
College 4-3 X:AST & ASE, X:ASG & C, X:C & BSG, ZONE: ASG & C	**Gap 8**
4-3 Eagle X:AST & ASE, X:ASG & C, X: C & BSG	**6-5 Goal Line**

Figure 4-4

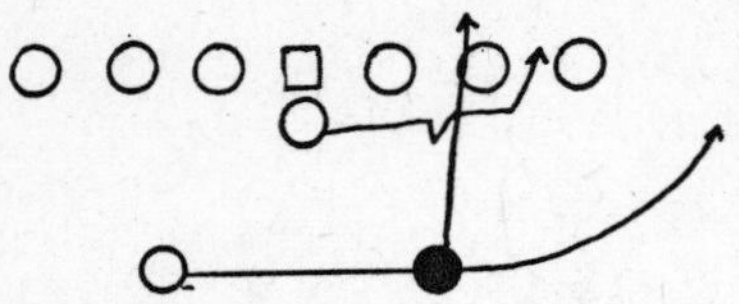	**Split Backs** Good dive option play. If this is the purpose of using Quick, change the ASE's rule to: EAGLE, DOWNFIELD.
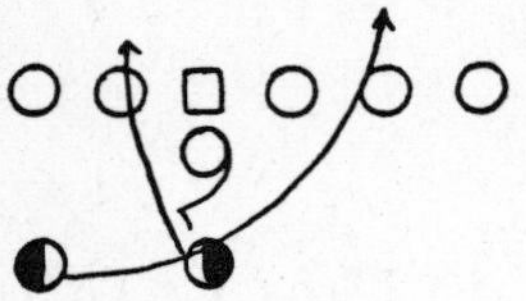	**Weak Backs** Good play, ball can be given to either back.
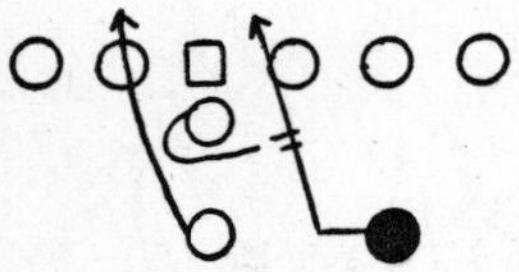	**Strong Backs** Good play, ball can be given to either back.
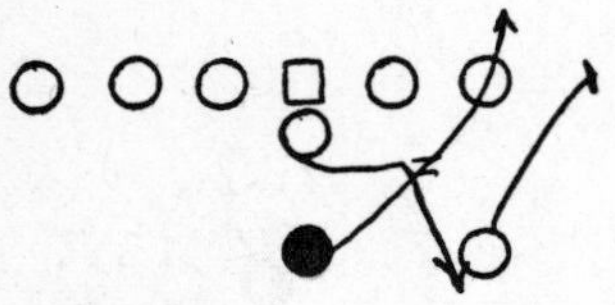	**Toward the X End** Good play versus seven-man fronts and most reduced eight-man fronts.
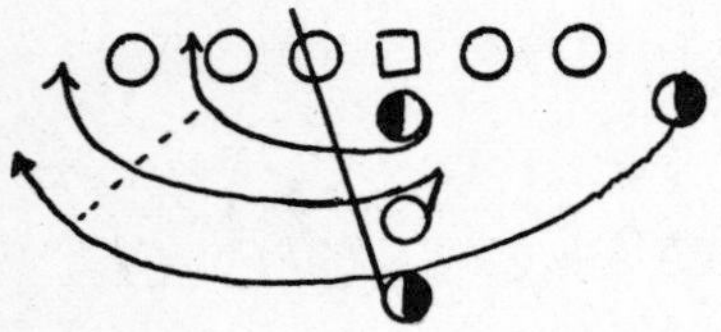	**Slotback** 1. Good scheme for the counter option (as diagrammed). If used for this purpose, change the ASE's rule to: EAGLE, DOWNFIELD. 2. Other backfield actions can be run toward or away from the slotback. If toward the slotback, he should block ASE rules.
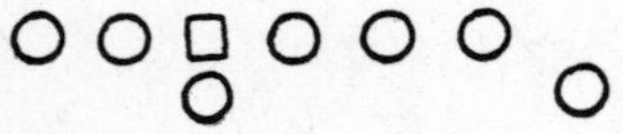	**Wingback** OK, but it is better to flank the wingback and spread the secondary.

VEER

Comments and Coaching Points

1. The Veer scheme should be used with the triple option play.
2. The squared defender represents the quarterback's dive read and the circled defender represents the quarterback's pitch key.
3. The triple option has been acclaimed by many as the greatest offensive innovation since the forward pass. It is a complete offensive play that attacks both the inside and outside sectors of the defense. Despite its advantages, however, it is a high-risk play and the defense is afforded the opportunity of punishing the fullback every time the play is initiated.

Figure 4-5

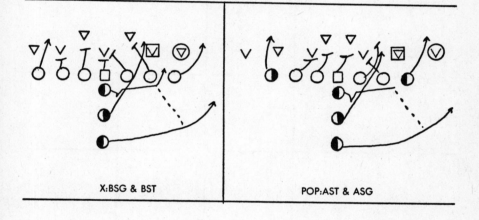

3-4   Split-4

X:BSG & BST   POP:AST & ASG

Figure 4-6

POSITIONS	RULE ASSIGNMENT			
ASE	DOWNFIELD			
AST	TANDEM, INSIDE, LINEBACKER			
ASG	STACK, ON, INSIDE, LINEBACKER			
C	RULE			
BSG	RULE			
BST	RULE			
BSE	DOWNFIELD			
POSITIONS	CROSSBLOCK	ZONE	POP	SCOOP
ASE & AST				
AST & ASG			Split-4	
ASG & C			5-3 5-3 Stack	
C & BSG	College 4-3 4-3 Eagle Weak Gap Stack			
BSG & BST	3-4 Strong Gap Stack 5-3 5-3 Stack			
OTHER				

Figure 4-7

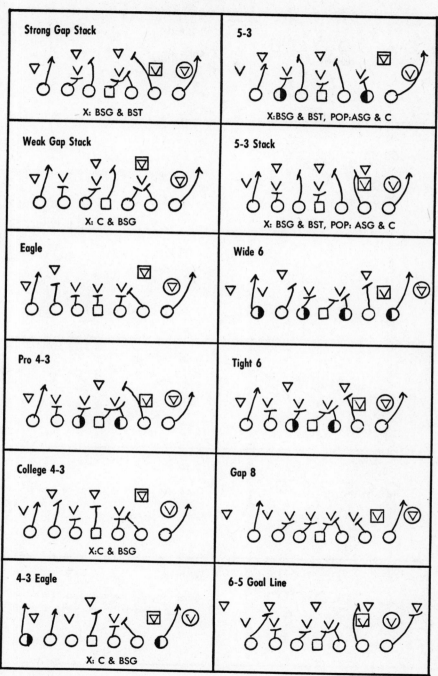

Figure 4-8

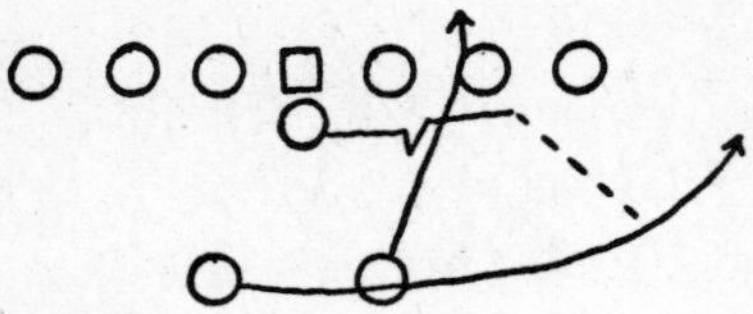

Split Backs

Good play.

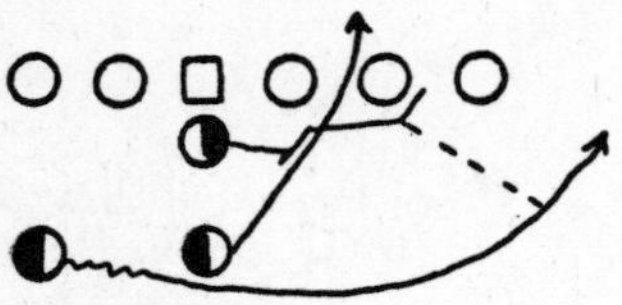

Weak Backs

Good play—the halfback should go in short motion to maintain a good pitch ratio with the quarterback.

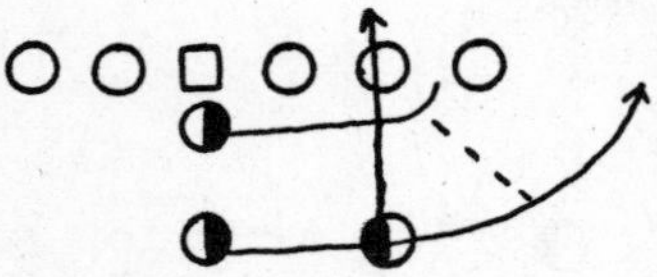

Strong Backs

Good play.

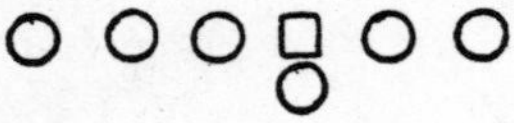

Toward the X End

Good play.

Slotback

Good play—the slotback can be used to add misdirection to the offense. When the Veer is run toward the slotback he should use ASE rules.

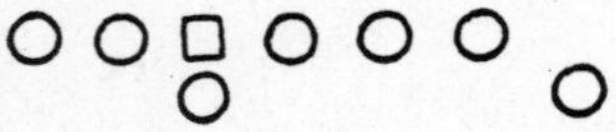

Wingback

Better to spread the defense out with a flanker than it is to cramp things up with a wingback.

OUTSIDE ICE

Comments and Coaching Points

1. The Outside Ice is a quick-hitting, straight-ahead power play, characterized by the isolation of an attackside linebacker by one of the running backs.

2. The difference between the Outside Ice and the Inside Ice is that if there is a defender aligned in the B gap, the Outside Ice will break outside of this defender and the Inside Ice will break inside of him.

3. Versus the 3-4 Defense, the ball carrier will key the defensive end. If this defender slants into the B gap, the ball carrier will break the play into the C gap, but if the defensive end holds ground or slants into the C gap, the ball carrier will follow the fullback and run through the A or B gaps.

4. The circled defender represents the linebacker to be blocked by the fullback.

Figure 4-9

3-4   Split-4

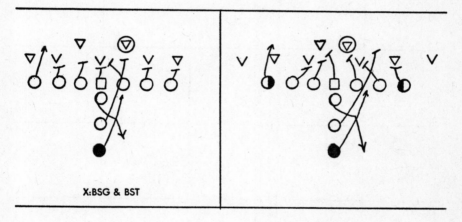

X:BSG & BST

Figure 4-10

POSITIONS	RULE ASSIGNMENT			
ASE	GAP, ON, OUTSIDE			
AST	ON, INSIDE, OUTSIDE			
ASG	STACK, ON, INSIDE, LINEBACKER			
C	ON, OVER, LINEBACKER			
BSG	RULE			
BST	RULE			
BSE	DOWNFIELD			
POSITIONS	CROSSBLOCK	ZONE	POP	SCOOP
ASE & AST				
AST & ASG				
ASG & C			5-3 5-3 Stack	
C & BSG	6-5 College 4-3 4-3 Eagle Pro 4-3 Wide 6 Tight 6			
BSG & BST	3-4 Strong Gap Stack 5-3 5-3 Stack			
OTHER				

Figure 4-11

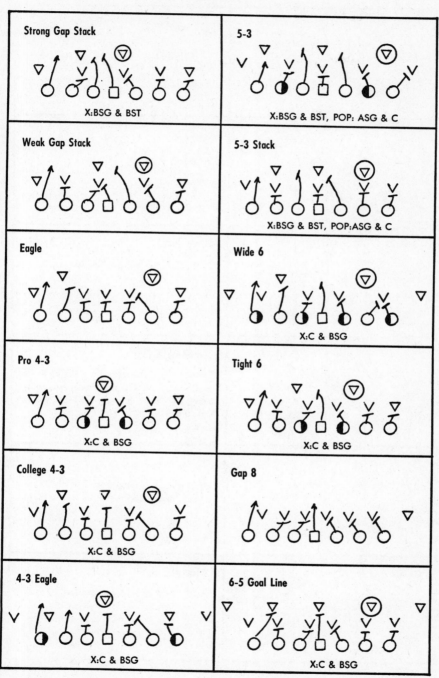

Figure 4-12

	Split Backs Good play.
	Weak Backs Good play.
	Strong Backs Good play—the halfback may have to cheat up slightly.
	Toward the X End Better to use the Inside Ice. The Outside Ice is only good toward the split end side versus the 3-4, Strong Gap Stack, Pro 4-3, 5-3 Stack, Wide 6, Tight 6 and 6-5.
	Slotback Good toward or away from the slot. If toward the slot, the slotback will block ASE rules.
	Wingback Good formation—the wingback can be used for misdirection.

INSIDE ICE

Comments and Coaching Points

1. The differences between the Inside Ice and the Outside Ice were noted in the preceding section. Both the Inside and Outside Ice can be used at any time, but they are most effective when the linebackers are playing loose.

2. If a coach wishes to incorporate both the Ice and the Iso Option, he should use Inside Ice rules.

3. Another advantage of the Inside Ice is that it can be effectively used toward the X end.

Figure 4-13

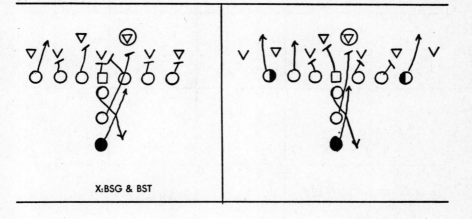

3-4   Split-4

X:BSG & BST

Figure 4-14

POSITIONS	RULE ASSIGNMENT			
ASE	DOWNFIELD			
AST	ON, OUTSIDE			
ASG	ON, REACH, STACK, INSIDE			
C	ON, OVER, LINEBACKER			
BSG	ON, OVER, BACKSIDE GAP			
BST	ON, OVER, LINEBACKER			
BSE	DOWNFIELD			
POSITIONS	CROSSBLOCK	ZONE	POP	SCOOP
ASE & AST				
AST & ASG				
ASG & C			5-3 Stack	
C & BSG	6-5 Weak Gap Stack Pro 4-3 College 4-3 4-3 Eagle Wide 6 Tight 6			
BSG & BST	3-4 5-3 Stack			
OTHER				

Figure 4-15

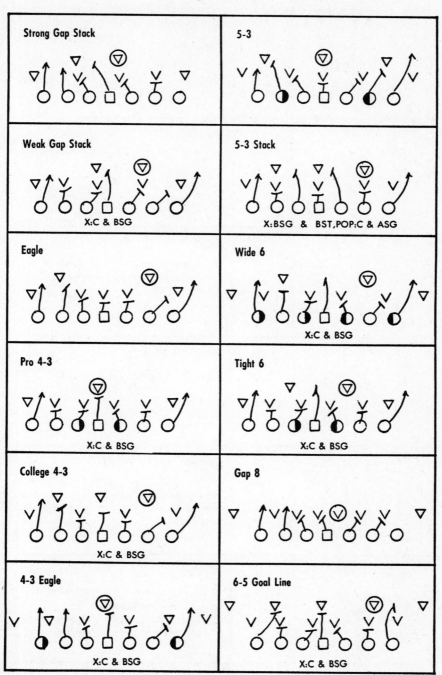

Figure 4-16

	Split Backs Good play.
	Weak Backs Good play
	Strong Backs Good play. If run from a full house (as diagrammed), the backside halfback can be used to run the Iso Option.
	Toward the X End Good play using all backfield sets.
	Slotback Good play toward or away from the slot. If toward the slot, he will block ASE rules. If run away from the slot, the slotback can be used to run the Iso Option.
	Wingback 1. Good play toward or away from the wing using any backfield set. 2. The wingback can be used as either a counter-threat, or as a decoy counter-threat.

TRAP

Comments and Coaching Points

1. This is the basic trap play. It is sound versus all defenses and easily adapts itself to any backfield set.
2. Traps are most effective versus hard-charging defensive lines.
3. The Trap hits slightly wider than the Gut.

Figure 4-17

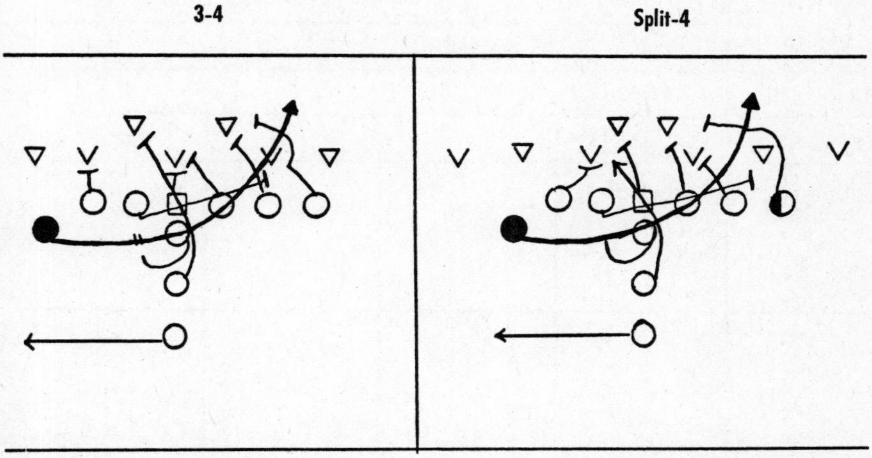

3-4   Split-4

Figure 4-18

POSITIONS	RULE ASSIGNMENT			
ASE	LINEBACKER			
AST	TANDEM, INSIDE, LINEBACKER			
ASG	ON, STACK, INSIDE, LINEBACKER			
C	BACKSIDE GAP, ON, OVER, AWAY			
BSG	FULL & TRAP			
BST	INSIDE, ON, LINEBACKER			
BSE	DOWNFIELD			
POSITIONS	CROSSBLOCK	ZONE	POP	SCOOP
ASE & AST				
AST & ASG				
ASG & C			5-3 5-3 Stack	
C & BSG				
BSG & BST				
OTHER				

Figure 4-19

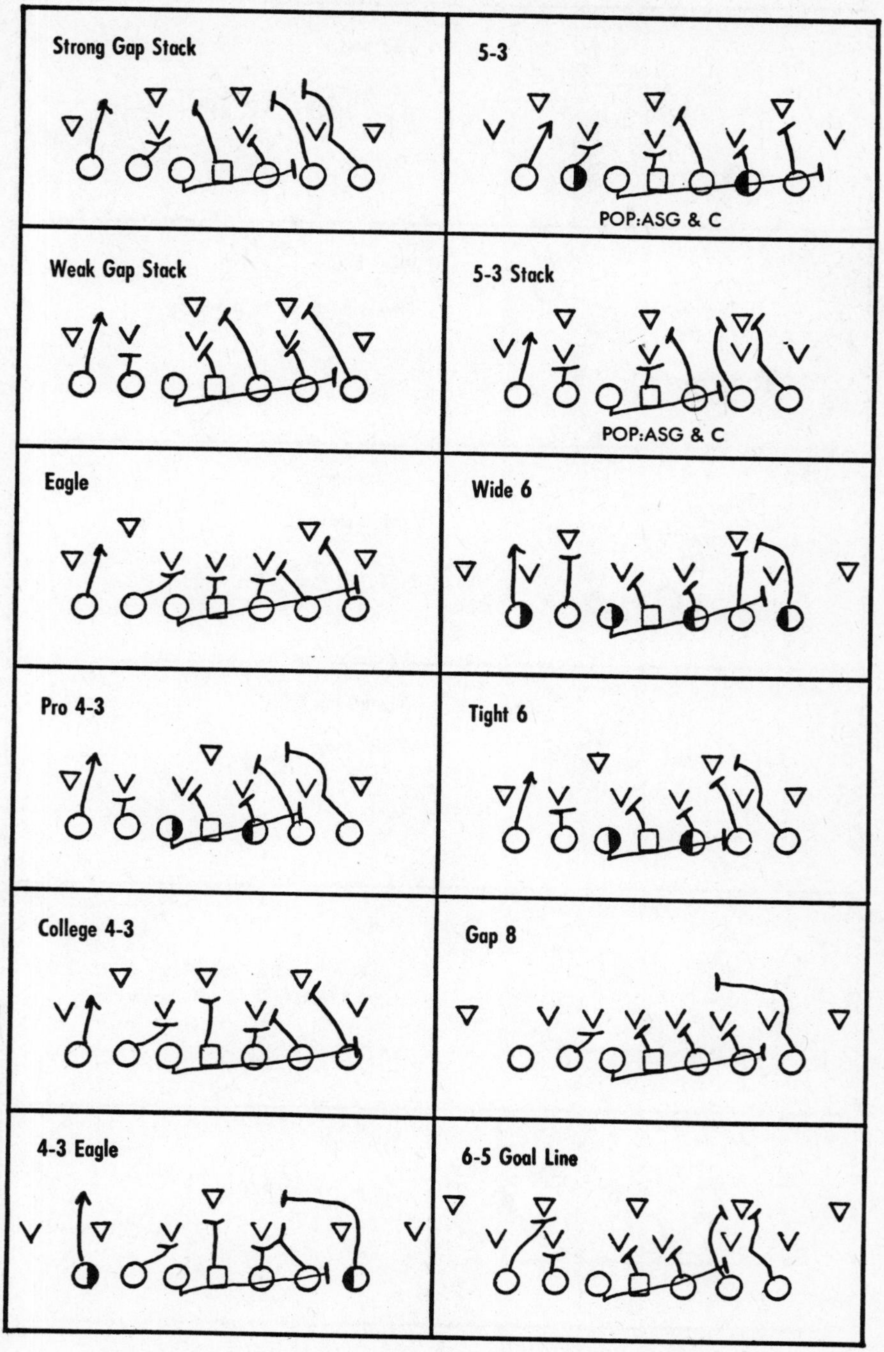

Strong Gap Stack	5-3
	POP:ASG & C
Weak Gap Stack	5-3 Stack
	POP:ASG & C
Eagle	Wide 6
Pro 4-3	Tight 6
College 4-3	Gap 8
4-3 Eagle	6-5 Goal Line

Figure 4-20

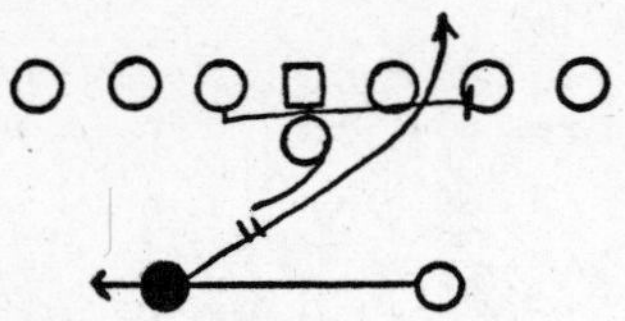	**Split Backs** Good play.
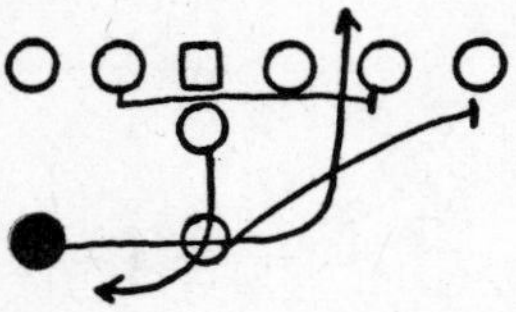	**Weak Backs** Fine addition to the power series.
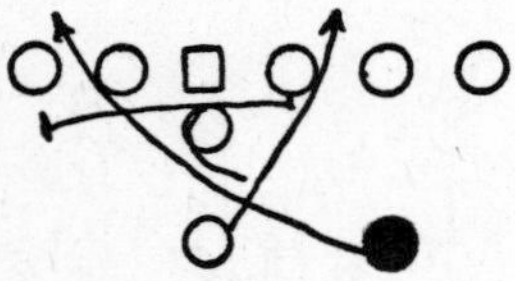	**Strong Backs** Good play.
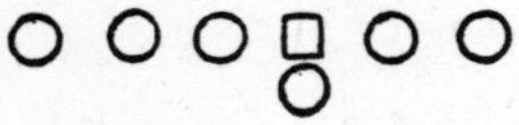	**Toward the X End** Good play
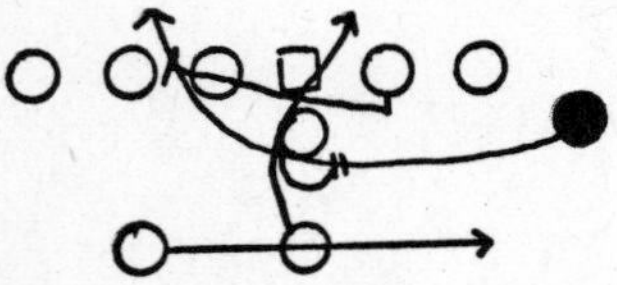	**Slotback** Excellent from the I (see Figure 4-17). Can also be used from a Slot-T (as diagrammed).
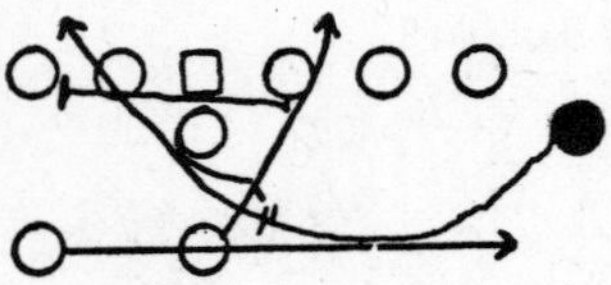	**Wingback** Good Winged-T play.

T-TRAP

Comments and Coaching Points

1. The main difference between the T-Trap and other traps is that the offensive tackle becomes the trapper. Obviously a fairly quick tackle is needed to make this play successful.

2. The T-Trap should be used with backfield actions that develop more slowly than the normal Trap.

3. The T-Trap is a more effective scheme versus the Split-4, and defenses in which the inside linebackers read the guards.

Figure 4-21

3-4   Split-4

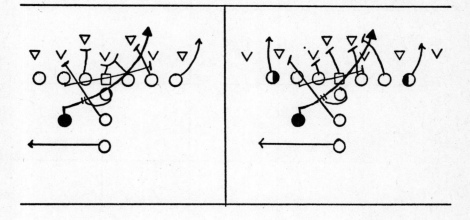

Figure 4-22

POSITIONS	RULE ASSIGNMENT			
ASE	DOWNFIELD			
AST	OVER, TANDEM, LINEBACKER			
ASG	GAP, STACK, INSIDE, LINEBACKER			
C	ON, OVER, AWAY			
BSG	ON, OVER, BACKSIDE GAP, GAP			
BST	PULL & TRAP			
BSE	DOWNFIELD			
POSITIONS	CROSSBLOCK	ZONE	POP	SCOOP
ASE & AST				
AST & ASG				
ASG & C			5-3 5-3 Stack	
C & BSG				
BSG & BST				
OTHER				

Figure 4-23

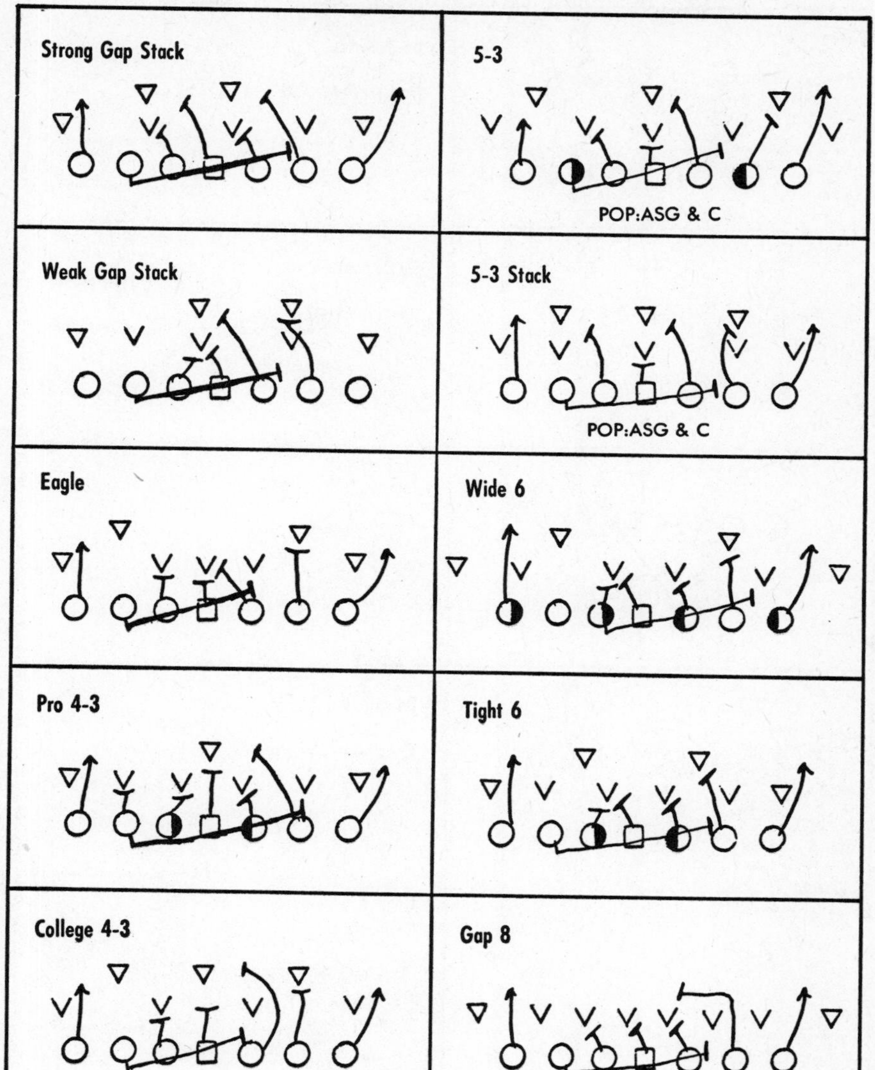

Strong Gap Stack

5-3

POP:ASG & C

Weak Gap Stack

5-3 Stack

POP:ASG & C

Eagle

Wide 6

Pro 4-3

Tight 6

College 4-3

Gap 8

4-3 Eagle

6-5 Goal Line

Figure 4-24

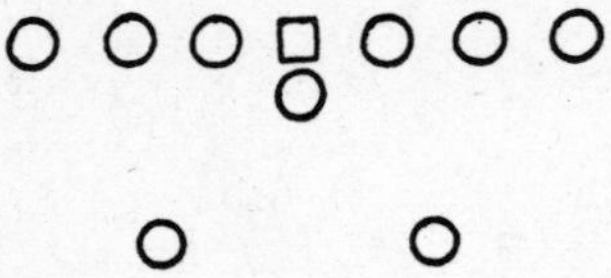	**Split Backs** Not a good play.
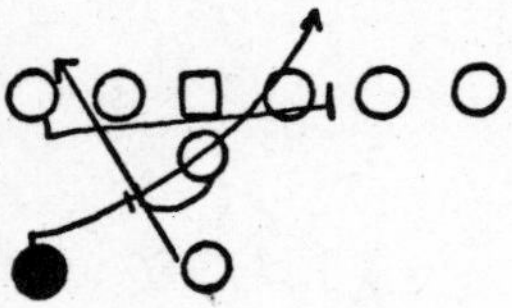	**Weak Backs** Excellent play.
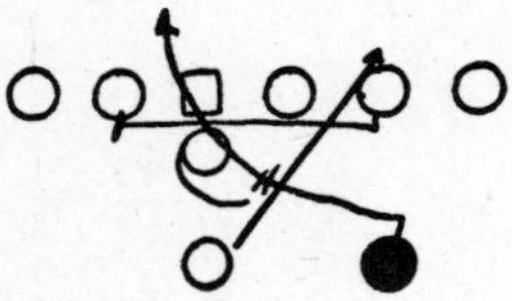	**Strong Backs** Excellent play.
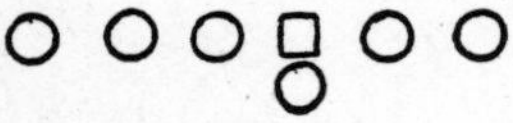	**Toward the X End** Excellent play from Strong Backs or the "I."
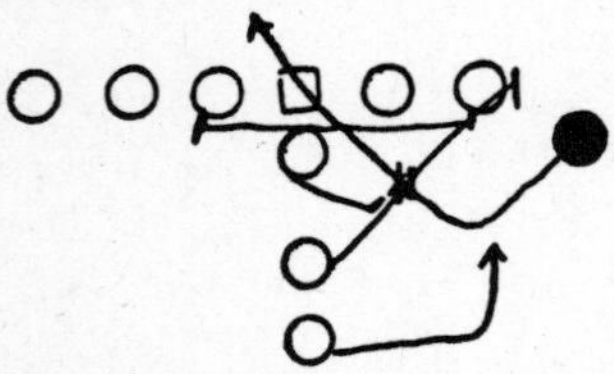	**Slotback** Another variation from the "I."
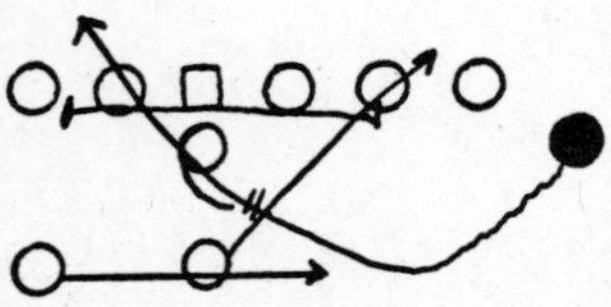	**Wingback** Excellent Winged-T play.

Y-TRAP

Comments and Coaching Points

1. The Y-Trap is used to engineer wingback counter-plays.
2. Although the Y-Trap was originally developed for the Winged-T offense, it adapts itself well to any backfield set that utilizes a wingback.
3. The main advantage of the Y-Trap is the lead block of the Y end.

Figure 4-25

3-4   Split-4

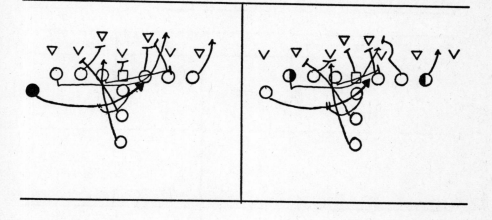

Figure 4-26

POSITIONS	RULE ASSIGNMENT
ASE	DOWNFIELD
AST	OVER, TANDEM, LINEBACKER
ASG	RULE
C	ON, AWAY
BSG	PULL & TRAP
BST	FILL
BSE	PULL & LEAD

POSITIONS	CROSSBLOCK	ZONE	POP	SCOOP
ASE & AST				
AST & ASG				
ASG & C			5-3 5-3 Stack	
C & BSG				
BSG & BST				
OTHER				

Figure 4-27

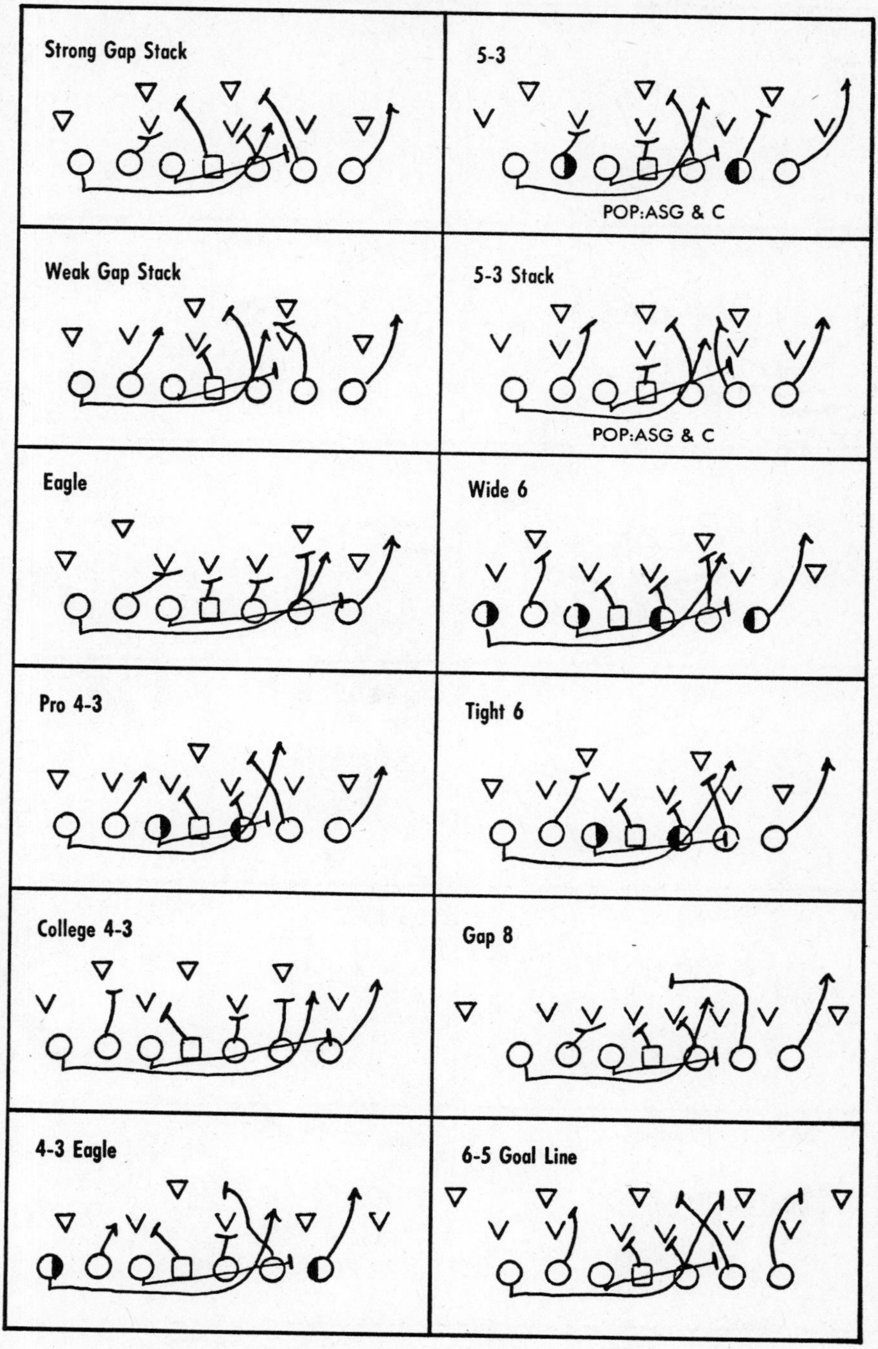

Strong Gap Stack

5-3

POP:ASG & C

Weak Gap Stack

5-3 Stack

POP:ASG & C

Eagle

Wide 6

Pro 4-3

Tight 6

College 4-3

Gap 8

4-3 Eagle

6-5 Goal Line

Figure 4-28

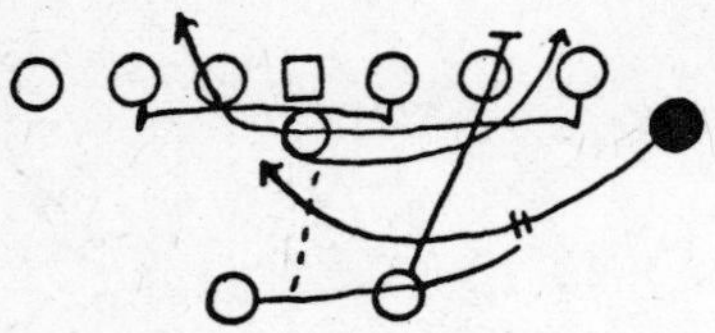	**Split Backs** Good play.
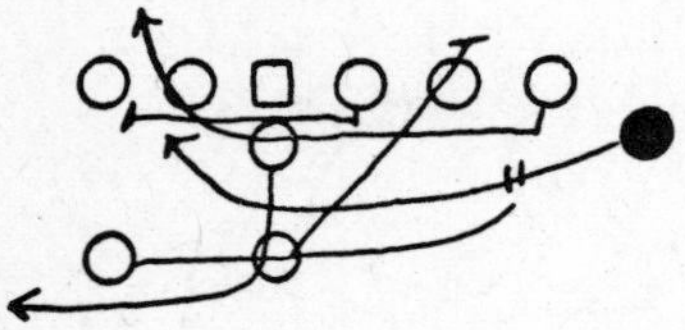	**Weak Backs** Excellent Winged-T play.
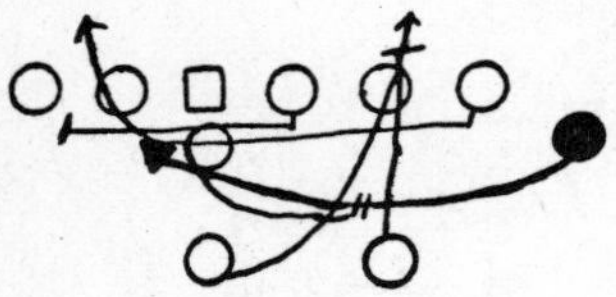	**Strong Backs** Good play, the fullback may have to cheat back slightly.
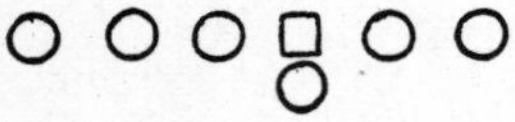	**Toward the X End** Excellent.
	**Slotback** Not a good play
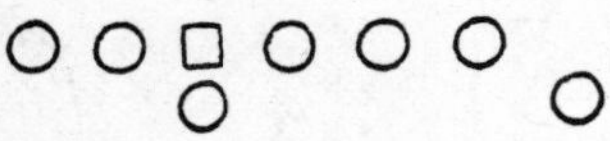	**Wingback** Used only from a wing.

GUT

Comments and Coaching Points

1. The Gut is the lead-off play of the Winged-T buck sweep series.
2. It easily adapts itself to any backfield set.
3. The Gut should be used with quick-hitting backfield actions that are directed inside of the B gaps.

Figure 4-29

3-4   Split-4

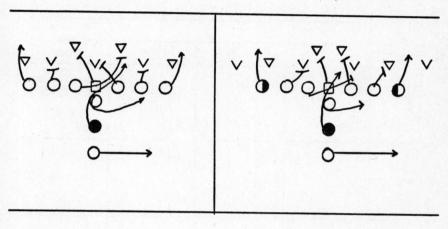

Figure 4-30

POSITIONS	RULE ASSIGNMENT			
ASE	DOWNFIELD			
AST	ON, OVER, OUTSIDE, LINEBACKER			
ASG	STACK, INSIDE, LINEBACKER			
C	BLOCK ON VERSUS STACK, OTHERWISE BLOCK AWAY			
BSG	PULL & TRAP			
BST	RULE			
BSE	DOWNFIELD			
POSITIONS	CROSSBLOCK	ZONE	POP	SCOOP
ASE & AST				
AST & ASG				
ASG & C			5-3 5-3 Stack	
C & BSG				
BSG & BST				
OTHER				

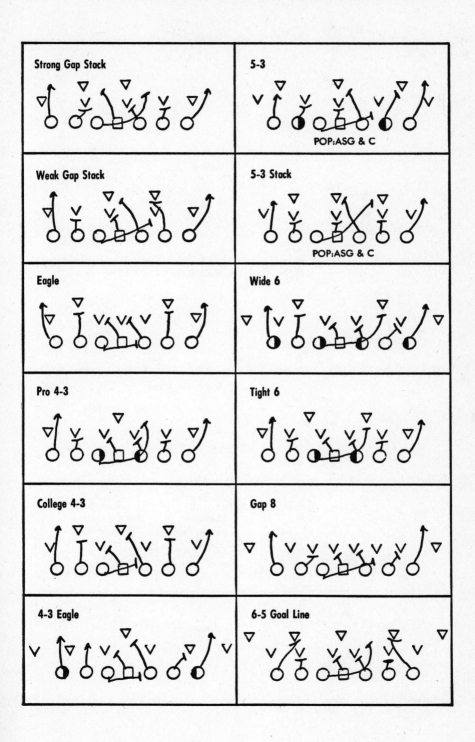

Figure 4-32

	Split Backs Good play—quarterback should fake quick pitch before handing off.
	Weak Backs Excellent Winged-T play. This is the lead-off for the buck sweep series.
	Strong Backs Good Split-T counter.
	Toward the X End Good play using any backfield set.
	Slotback Good play. By sending the slotback into quick motion, the Winged-T buck sweep series can be created.
	Wingback Excellent.

SQUEEZE

Comments and Coaching Points

1. The Squeeze is a variation of the basic trap. It hits slightly wider against some defensive sets.

2. The squeeze is specifically designed for slotback counter-plays, but can also be used with halfback counters.

3. Like the Y-Trap, the main advantage of the squeeze is the utilization of a lead blocker (the backside tackle).

4. The Squeeze puts tremendous pressure on the defensive tackle and inside linebacker. Because the initial blocking pattern resembles the Slant, Punch and Stampede, these players may be slow to react.

Figure 4-33

3-4   Split-4

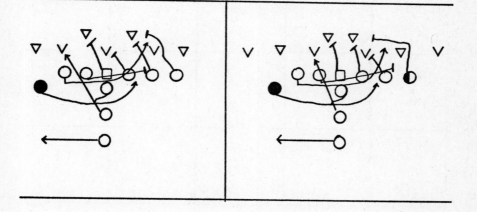

Figure 4-34

POSITIONS	RULE ASSIGNMENT			
ASE	INFLUENCE INSIDE & BLOCK: TANDEM, LINEBACKER			
AST	INSIDE, LINEBACKER			
ASG	INSIDE, LINEBACKER			
C	AWAY			
BSG	PULL & TRAP			
BST	PULL & LEAD			
BSE	DOWNFIELD			
POSITIONS	CROSSBLOCK	ZONE	POP	SCOOP
ASE & AST				
AST & ASG				
ASG & C				
C & BSG				
BSG & BST				
OTHER				

Figure 4-35

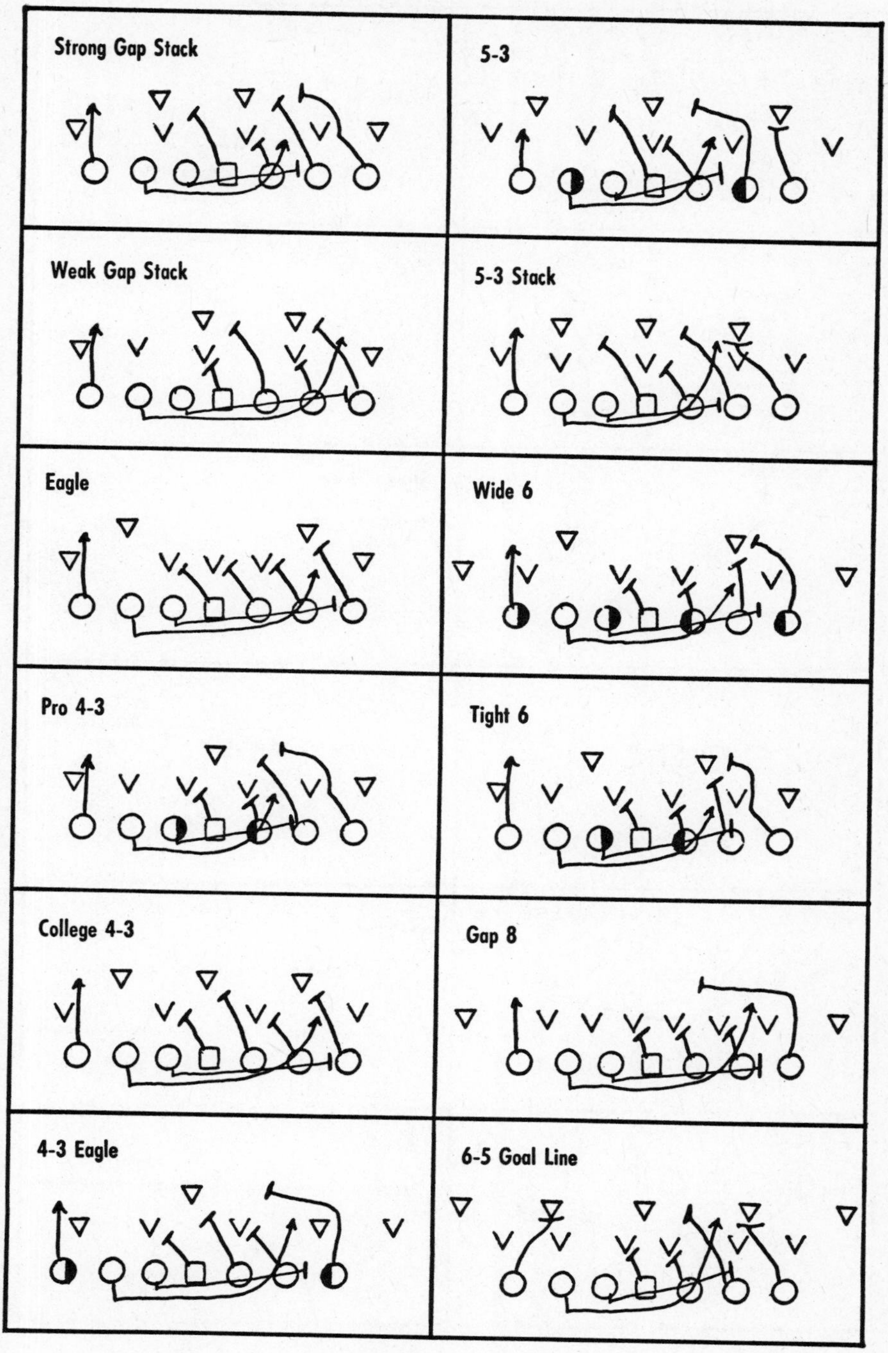
Strong Gap Stack
5-3
Weak Gap Stack
5-3 Stack
Eagle
Wide 6
Pro 4-3
Tight 6
College 4-3
Gap 8
4-3 Eagle
6-5 Goal Line

Figure 4-36

	Split Backs See Slotback.
	Weak Backs Excellent.
	Strong Backs Excellent.
	Toward the X End Better to use Trap rules for this purpose.
	Slotback Good counter-play for the veer offense.
	Wingback Excellent play—wingback must go into quick motion.

REACH

In Chapter 3, we discussed how and why Reach and Seal are used for plays directed intc the off-tackle hole. Reach can also be used for plays that attack the inside sector. The assignments and reasons for using Reach in the inside sector are identical to those listed in the preceding chapter. Figure 4-37 illustrates four plays utilizing Reach.

Figure 4-37

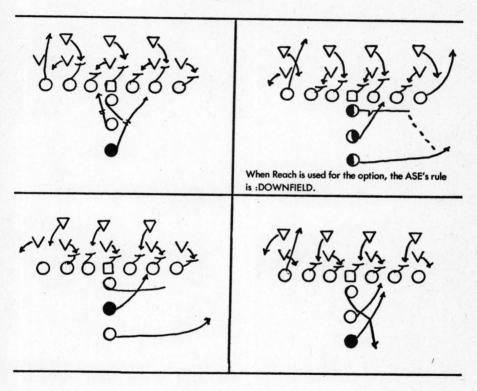

When Reach is used for the option, the ASE's rule is :DOWNFIELD.

5

Master Calls That Attack the Perimeter of Modern Defenses

SWEEP

Comments and Coaching Points

1. Sweep blocking should be used in conjunction with "USC student body right or left" type plays.
2. The sweep is probably the finest play to come from the "I" formation. Although it adapts to other formations, it is the trademark of almost every "I" team.
3. Speed, downfield blocking and the back's ability to find daylight are the main ingredients of the play.

Figure 5-1

3-4   Split-4

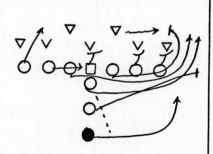 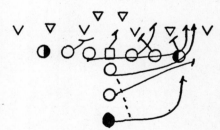

Note: When used with the "I" formation, the backside A gap need not be protected. The BSG could thus pull.

Figure 5-2

POSITIONS	RULE ASSIGNMENT
ASE	GAP, ON, OVER, OUTSIDE
AST	RULE
ASG	ON, PULL & BLOCK THE ATTACKSIDE LINEBACKER
C	RULE
BSG	GAP, PULL & LEAD
BST	FILL
BSE	DOWNFIELD

POSITIONS	CROSSBLOCK	ZONE	POP	SCOOP
ASE & AST				
AST & ASG				
ASG & C				
C & BSG	Weak Gap Stack			
BSG & BST				
OTHER				

Figure 5-3

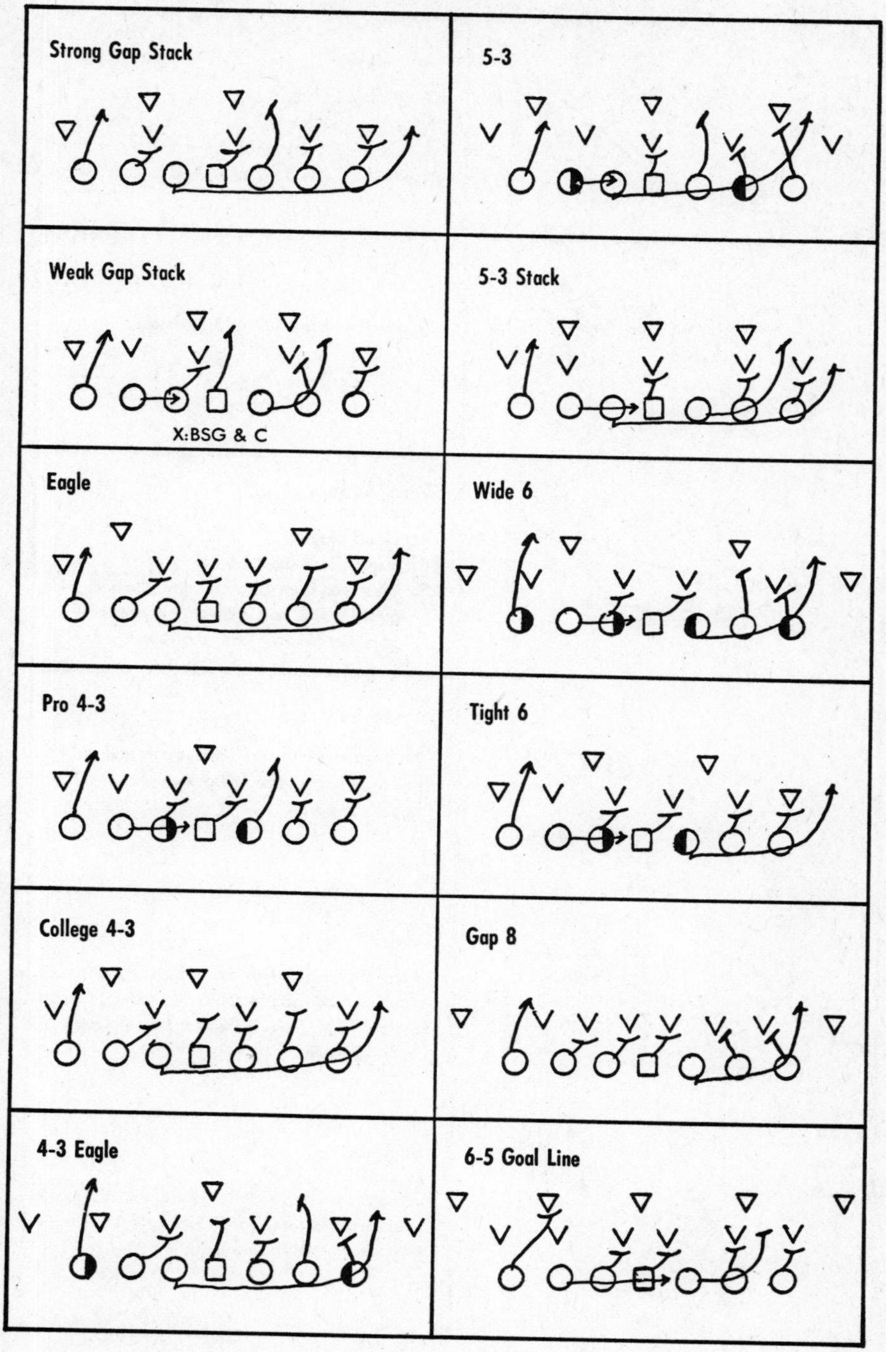

Strong Gap Stack

5-3

Weak Gap Stack

X:BSG & C

5-3 Stack

Eagle

Wide 6

Pro 4-3

Tight 6

College 4-3

Gap 8

4-3 Eagle

6-5 Goal Line

Figure 5-4

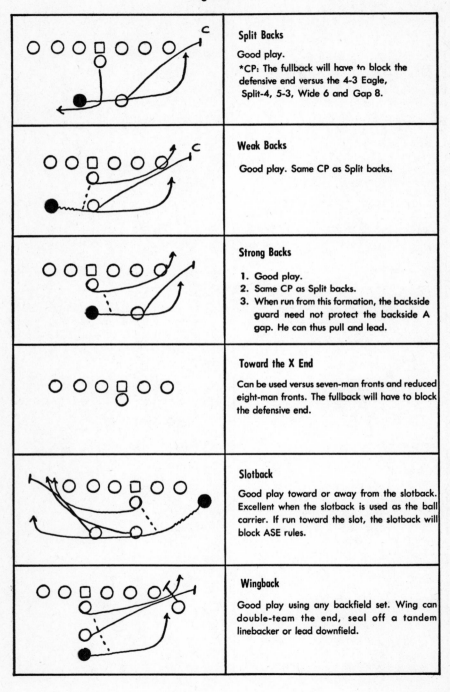

Split Backs

Good play.

*CP: The fullback will have to block the defensive end versus the 4-3 Eagle, Split-4, 5-3, Wide 6 and Gap 8.

Weak Backs

Good play. Same CP as Split backs.

Strong Backs

1. Good play.
2. Same CP as Split backs.
3. When run from this formation, the backside guard need not protect the backside A gap. He can thus pull and lead.

Toward the X End

Can be used versus seven-man fronts and reduced eight-man fronts. The fullback will have to block the defensive end.

Slotback

Good play toward or away from the slotback. Excellent when the slotback is used as the ball carrier. If run toward the slot, the slotback will block ASE rules.

Wingback

Good play using any backfield set. Wing can double-team the end, seal off a tandem linebacker or lead downfield.

Y-SWEEP

Comments and Coaching Points

1. The Y-Sweep is a variation of the regular Sweep. It differs in that the Y end will block downfield versus many defenses.
2. The outside linebacker will either be blocked by a wingback or a lead back.
3. Depending upon the outside linebacker's reaction to the play, it may break through either the C or D gaps.
4. If the outside linebacker has been taught to "chug" the Y end, the Y-Sweep will put him in an assignment conflict.

Figure 5-5

3-4   Split-4

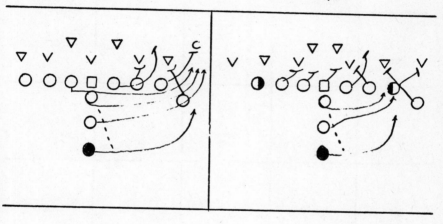

Figure 5-6

POSITIONS	RULE ASSIGNMENT			
ASE	TANDEM, OUTSIDE, DOWNFIELD			
AST	RULE			
ASG	ON, PULL & BLOCK THE ATTACKSIDE LINEBACKER			
C	RULE			
BSG	GAP, PULL & LEAD			
BST	FILL			
BSE	DOWNFIELD			
POSITIONS	CROSSBLOCK	ZONE	POP	SCOOP
ASE & AST				
AST & ASG				
ASG & C				
C & BSG	Weak Gap Stack			
BSG & BST				
OTHER				

Figure 5-7

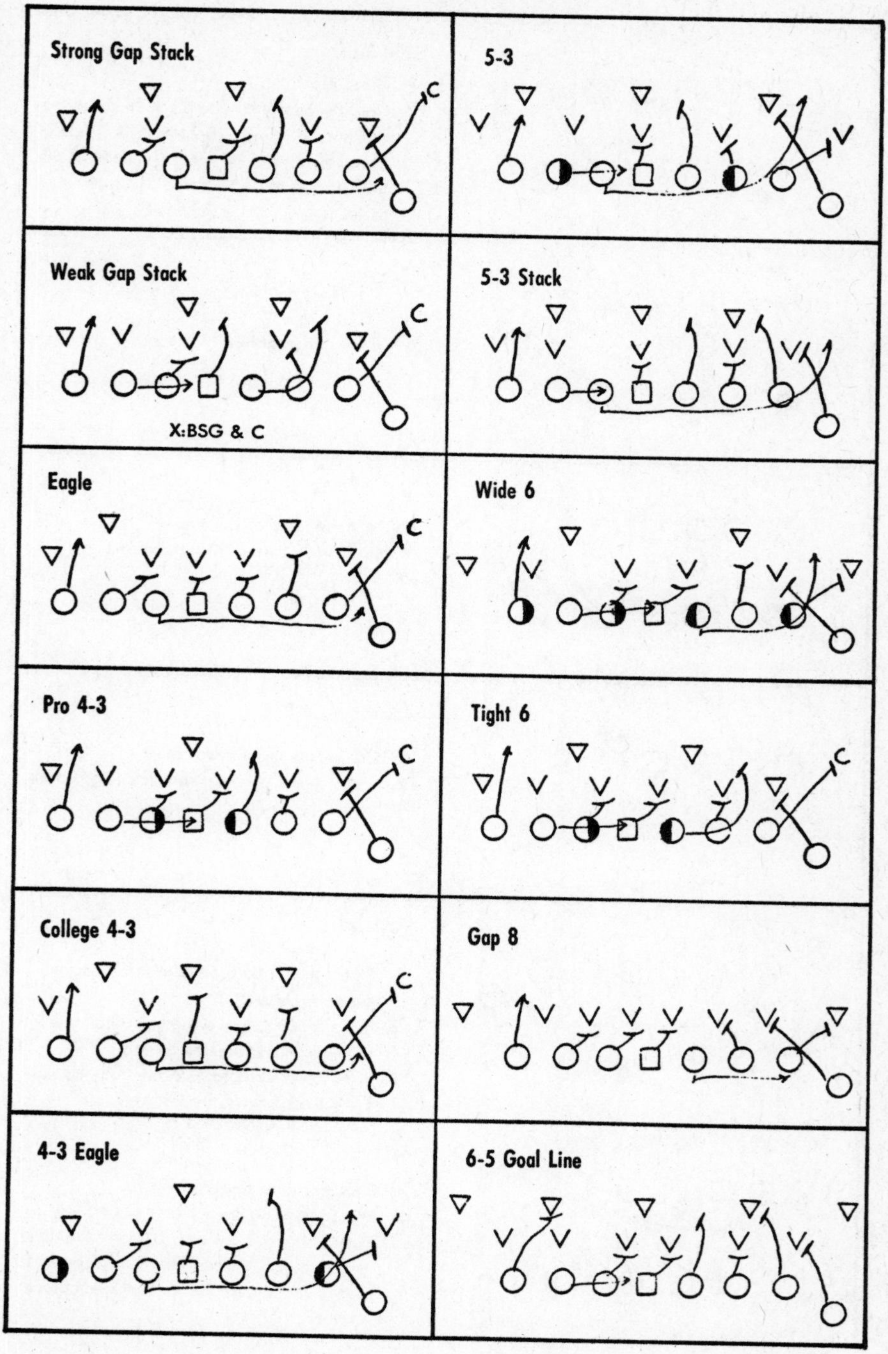
Strong Gap Stack
5-3
Weak Gap Stack
5-3 Stack
X:BSG & C
Eagle
Wide 6
Pro 4-3
Tight 6
College 4-3
Gap 8
4-3 Eagle
6-5 Goal Line

Figure 5-8

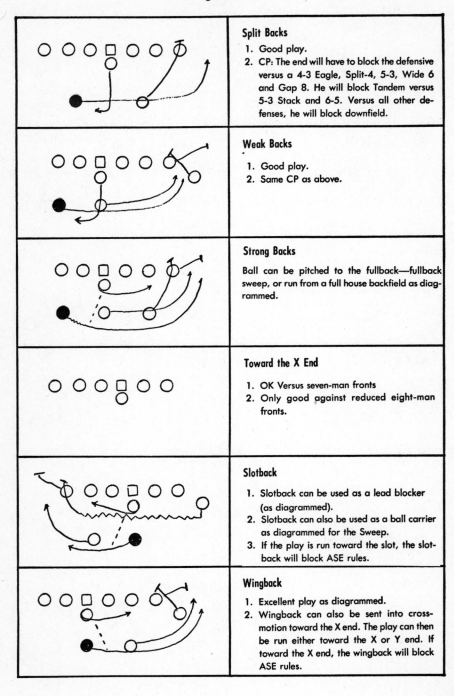

Split Backs

1. Good play.
2. CP: The end will have to block the defensive versus a 4-3 Eagle, Split-4, 5-3, Wide 6 and Gap 8. He will block Tandem versus 5-3 Stack and 6-5. Versus all other defenses, he will block downfield.

Weak Backs

1. Good play.
2. Same CP as above.

Strong Backs

Ball can be pitched to the fullback—fullback sweep, or run from a full house backfield as diagrammed.

Toward the X End

1. OK Versus seven-man fronts
2. Only good against reduced eight-man fronts.

Slotback

1. Slotback can be used as a lead blocker (as diagrammed).
2. Slotback can also be used as a ball carrier as diagrammed for the Sweep.
3. If the play is run toward the slot, the slotback will block ASE rules.

Wingback

1. Excellent play as diagrammed.
2. Wingback can also be sent into cross-motion toward the X end. The play can then be run either toward the X or Y end. If toward the X end, the wingback will block ASE rules.

STAMPEDE

Comments and Coaching Points

1. The Stampede becomes an extremely effective play after the Punch, Squeeze or Slant has been established.

2. Versus all seven-man fronts (except the 4-3 Eagle) and the Tight 6 and 6-5 defenses, the ASG will block the cornerback (Strong safety if a flanker is used). The circled defender will thus be blocked by a wingback or lead back.

3. Versus the 4-3 Eagle, the Split-4, the 5-3, Wide 6 and Gap 8 defenses, the ASG will trap the end and the play will probably break through the D gap.

4. Versus the 5-3 Stack and 6-5 defenses, a leadback can be used to block the tandem linebacker, or this can be done by the backside guard.

Figure 5-9

3-4   Split-4

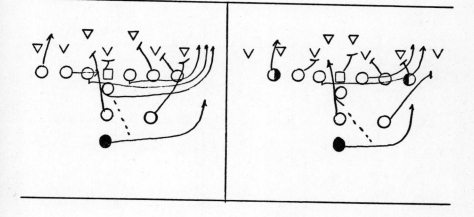

Figure 5-10

POSITIONS	RULE ASSIGNMENT			
ASE	INSIDE, LINEBACKER			
AST	INSIDE, LINEBACKER			
ASG	PULL & LEAD			
C	RULE			
BSG	PULL & LEAD			
BST	FILL			
BSE	DOWNFIELD			
POSITIONS	CROSSBLOCK	ZONE	POP	SCOOP
ASE & AST				
AST & ASG				
ASG & C				
C & BSG				
BSG & BST				
OTHER				

Figure 5-11

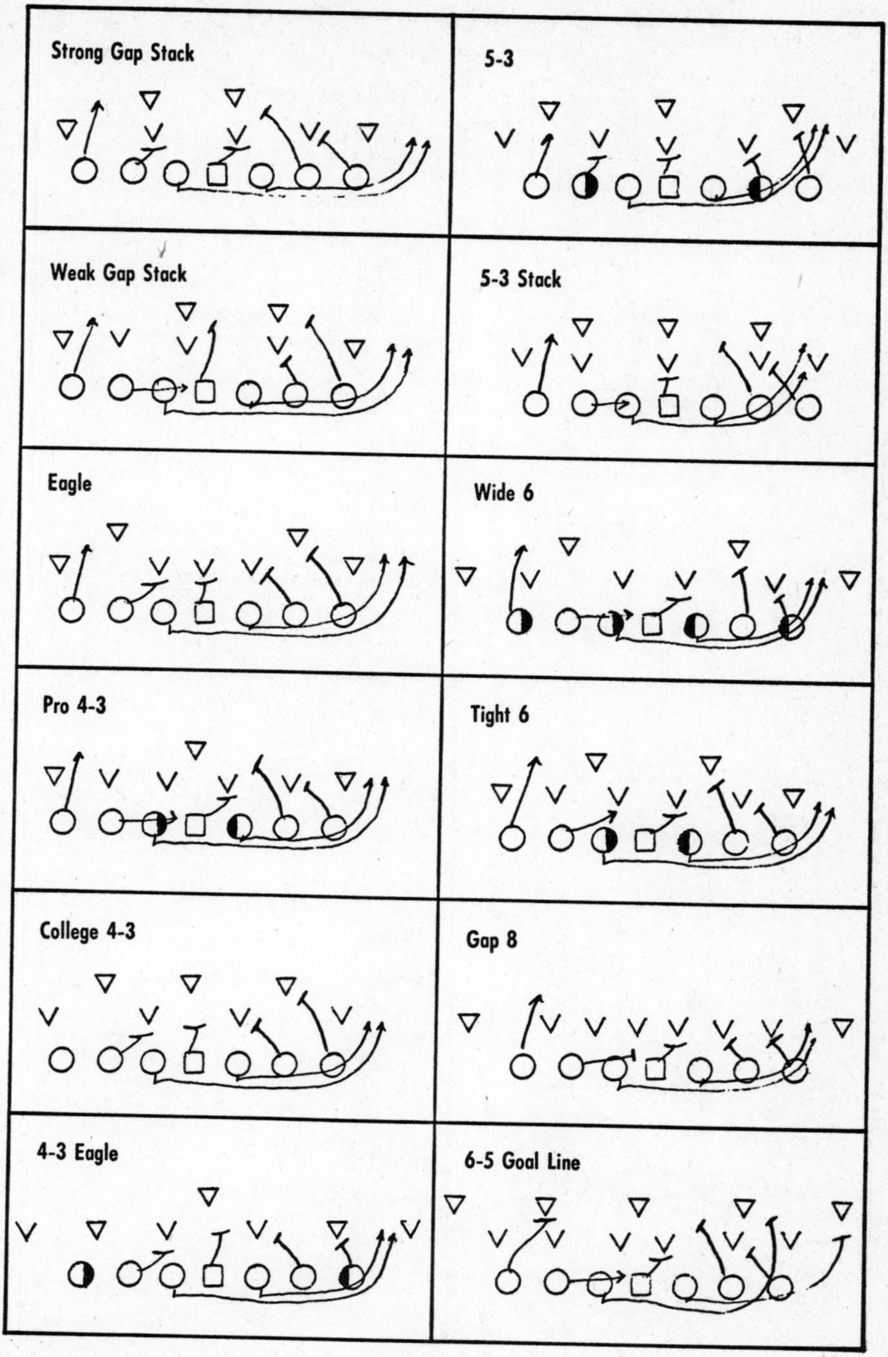
Strong Gap Stack
5-3
Weak Gap Stack
5-3 Stack
Eagle
Wide 6
Pro 4-3
Tight 6
College 4-3
Gap 8
4-3 Eagle
6-5 Goal Line

Figure 5-12

	Split Backs Only good with a wing.
	Weak Backs Good play if run toward a wing, or used with a full house backfield.
	Strong Backs Good play. Even if there is a defender in the backside A gap, he will have to be ultra quick to catch the fullback from behind.
	Toward the X End Not a good play.
	Slotback Great play. Another variation from the "I."
	Wingback Great play. Another variation of the "I."

PACKER

Comments and Coaching Points

1. Packer is a variation of the Green Bay Sweep. It is very effective versus the Pro 4-3 and is an ideal play for the Split back, pro offense.
2. A lead back will block the circled defender and the attackside guard will pull and block the cornerback (Strong safety if a flanker is used), or the defensive end, depending upon the defense.
3. Packer can be used in conjunction with the Punch, Stampede, Squeeze and Trap.

Figure 5-13

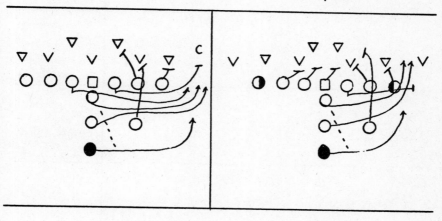

Figure 5-14

POSITIONS	RULE ASSIGNMENT			
ASE	GAP, ON, OVER, OUTSIDE			
AST	TANDEM, INSIDE, LINEBACKER			
ASG	PULL & TRAP THE FIRST DEFENDER OUTSIDE OF Y			
C	RULE			
BSG	GAP, PULL & LEAD			
BST	FILL			
BSE	DOWNFIELD			

POSITIONS	CROSSBLOCK	ZONE	POP	SCOOP
ASE & AST				
AST & ASG				
ASG & C				
C & BSG	Weak Gap Stack			
BSG & BST				
OTHER				

Figure 5-15

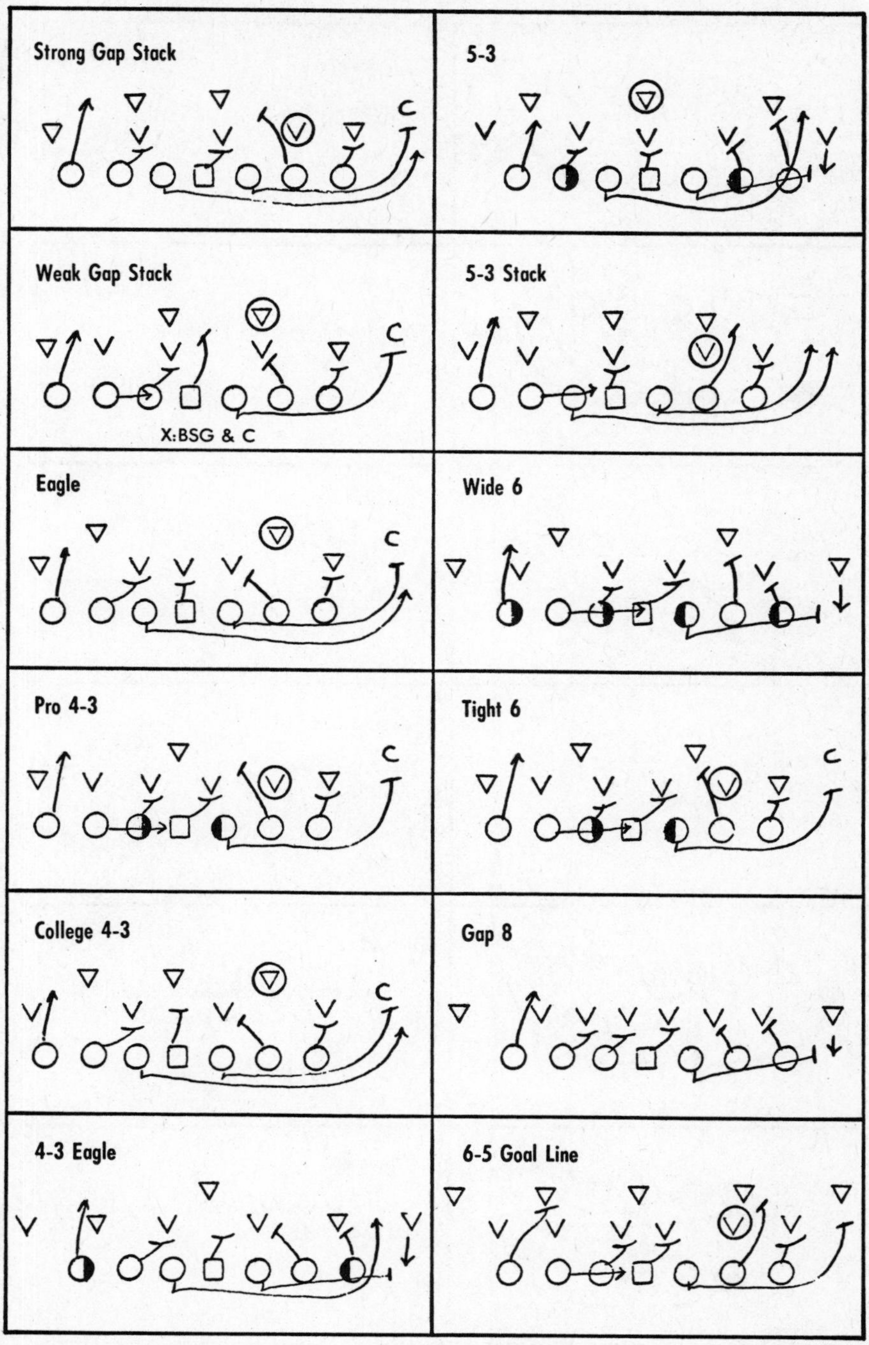
Strong Gap Stack
5-3
Weak Gap Stack
5-3 Stack
X:BSG & C
Eagle
Wide 6
Pro 4-3
Tight 6
College 4-3
Gap 8
4-3 Eagle
6-5 Goal Line

Figure 5-16

	Split Backs Good play.
	Weak Backs Only good from a full house backfield.
	Strong Backs Good play
	Toward the X End Not a good play.
	Slotback Good play as diagrammed. If directed toward the slot, the slotback will block ASE rules.
	Wingback Good play—the wingback can double-team the end or lead downfield.

REVERSE

Comments and Coaching Points

1. The Reverse, or end around, is most effective against quick-pursuing defenses.
2. The ball must be pitched deep to the ball carrier, to prevent him from getting caught up in the penetration.
3. The Reverse is not a bread-and-butter play. At most, it is used two or three times a game. It can result in a big gainer, but its success is really a "hit and miss" proposition.
4. Speed at the Split end position is essential for the play's success.

Figure 5-17

3-4

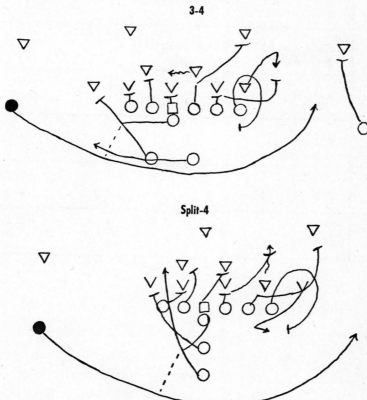

Split-4

Figure 5-18

RADAR BLOCKING

MASTER CALL: <u>REVERSE</u>   ATTACK AREA: <u>D GAP</u>

POSITION	BLOCKING ASSIGNMENT	ILLUSTRATED ASSIGNMENTS
ASE	RELEASE OUTSIDE & PEEL BACK (See illustration)	
AST	OUTSIDE GAP, ON, OVER, RELEASE FLAT (See illustration)	
ASG	REACH, ON, OVER, RELEASE DOWNFIELD (See illustration)	
C	RULE	
BSG	RULE	
BST	RULE	
BSE	DOWNFIELD	

Figure 5-19

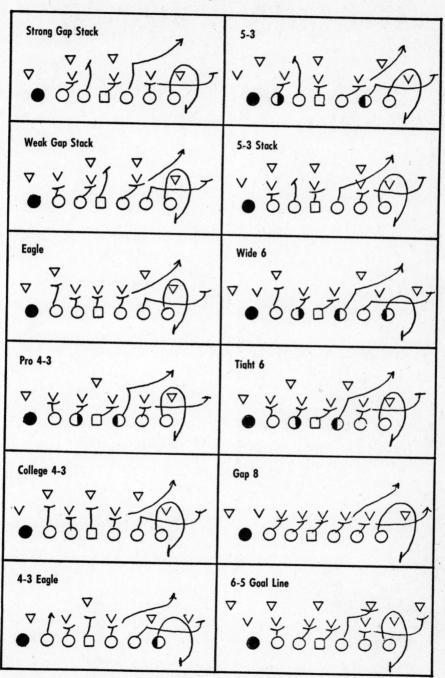

QUICK PITCH

Comments and Coaching Points

1. This play should be run from split or off backs.

2. The Quick pitch is extremely effective versus ends who crash hard to stop the option, or off-tackle plays.

3. We prefer to run this play from a Pro formation versus seven-man fronts and from a Twins formation versus eight-man fronts.

4. Defenders aligned in the attackside B gap are left unblocked. If the ball carrier is not fast enough to outrun this defender, the Quick Pitch should not be used.

Figure 5-20

3-4

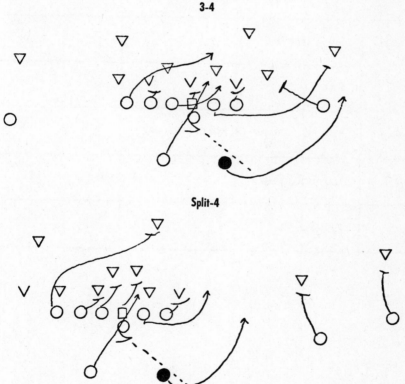

Split-4

Figure 5-21

RADAR BLOCKING

MASTER CALL: <u>QUICK PITCH</u>   ATTACK AREA: <u>D GAP</u>

POSITION	BLOCKING ASSIGNMENT	POSSIBLE COMBO CALL
ASE	PRO-LINEBACKER TWINS-STALK	
AST	ON, OUTSIDE	
ASG	PULL & LEAD	
C	RULE	
BSG	GAP, PULL THROUGH THE ATTACKSIDE A GAP	
BST	GAP, DOWNFIELD	
BSE	DOWNFIELD	

Figure 5-22

Quick Pitch Versus Eight-Man Fronts

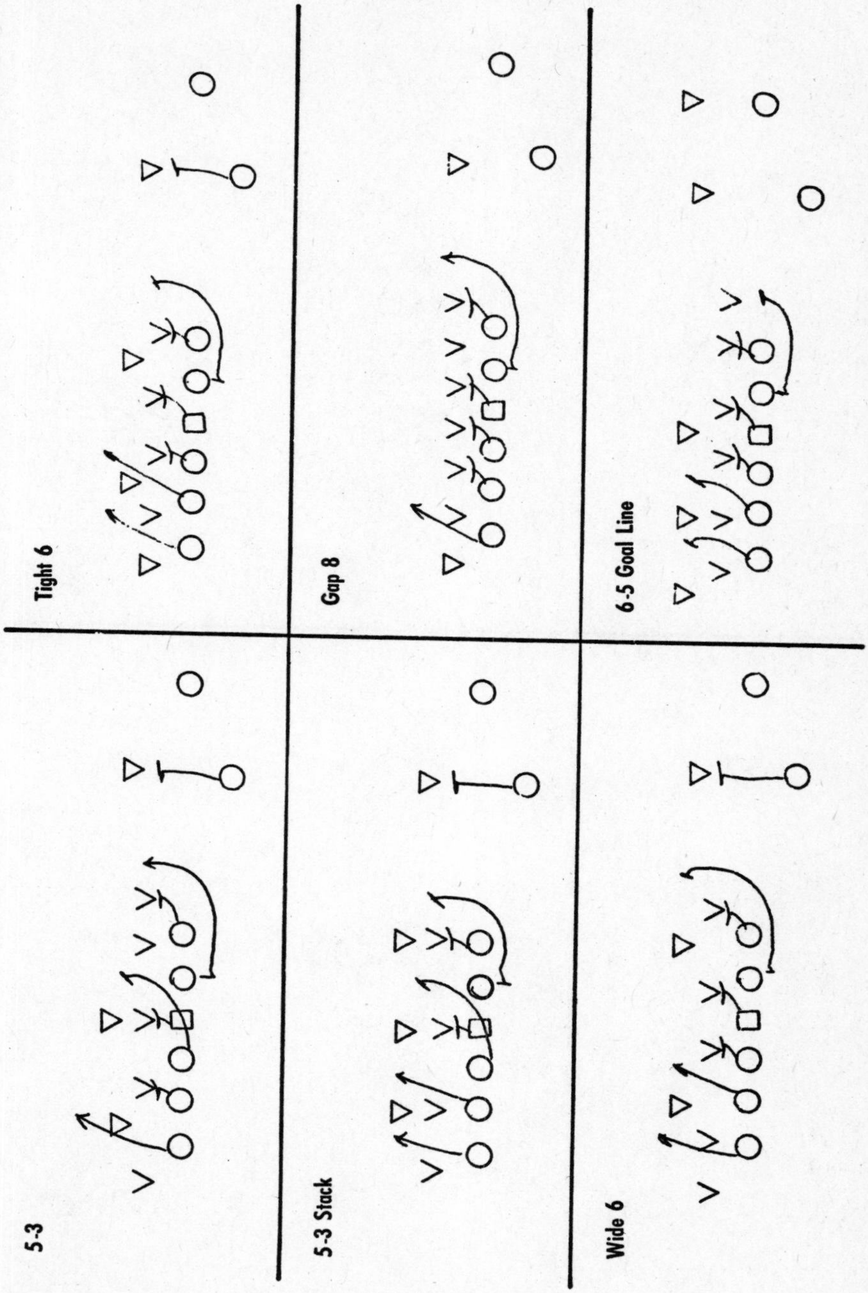

Figure 5-23

Quick Pitch Versus Seven-Man Fronts

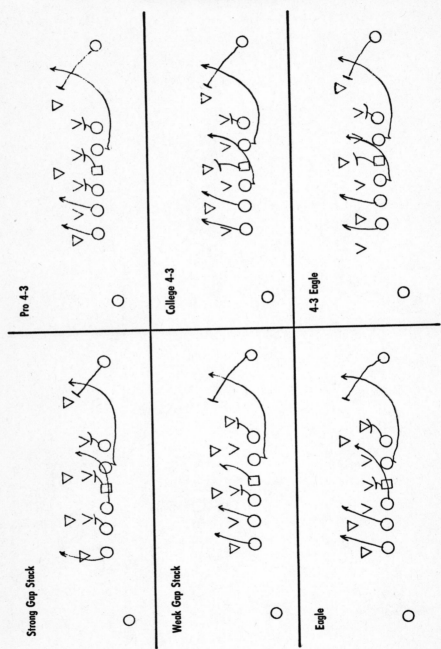

REACH

Reach can also be used for plays directed to the outside. Reach should be used in the same manner as described in Chapters 3 and 4. Figure 5-24 illustrates how Reach can be used with all four backfield sets.

Figure 5-24

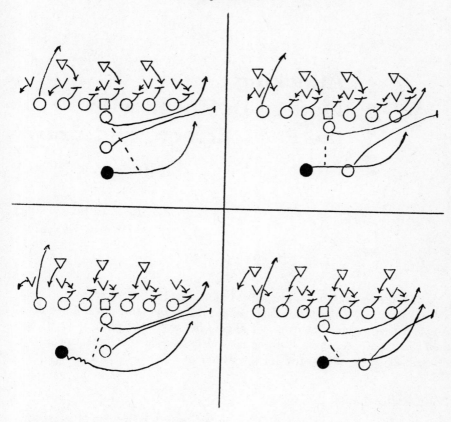

6

Attacking
Modern Defenses with
the Pass, Screen, and Draw

DROPBACK PROTECTION

We use three different methods of protecting the dropback passer. These are: (1) Solid, (2) Fan and (3) Dual. Which method is selected for a particular play is dependent upon the defensive alignment (seven- or eight-man front), the total number of receivers we wish to involve in the pattern and the depth of the quarterback's drop (three, five, or seven steps).

Solid Protection

Solid protection is man-for-man protection. Each lineman is assigned a defender and he stays with this defender until the play ends. The exception to this is when a lineman is assigned to block a linebacker. If his assigned linebacker drops off into coverage, the offensive lineman is free to help one of his teammates.

The purpose of Solid protection is to insure maximum protection. All five interior linemen have the same blocking rule, which is: On, Backside Gap, Hunt. Because we use the term Backside Gap, linemen must be told whether the protection is "Solid Right" or "Solid Left." Figure 6-1 illustrates solid protection versus 14 defenses. Upon examination of this chart, it becomes obvious that

142

Figure 6-1—Master Call: Solid Protection

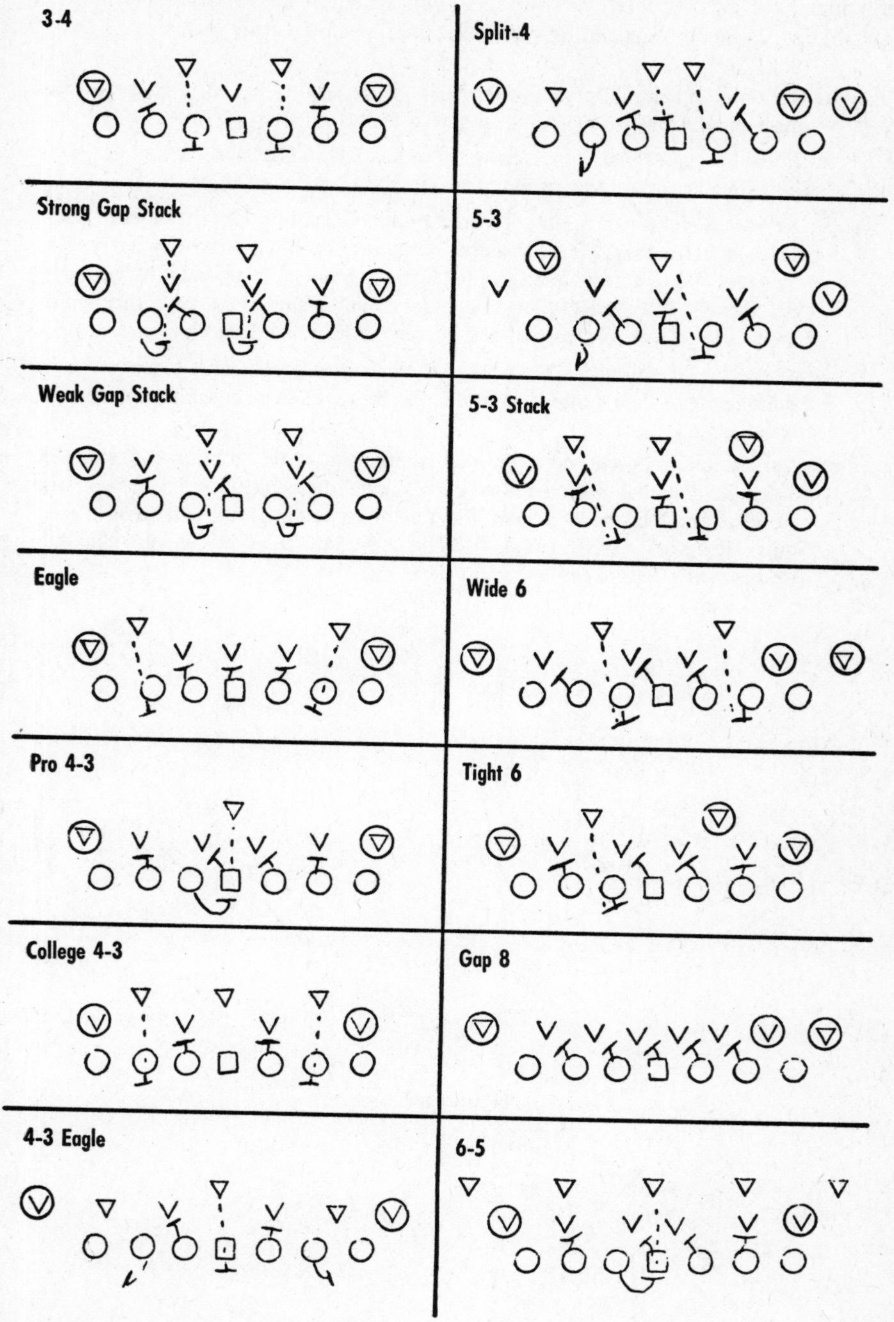

3-4

Split-4

Strong Gap Stack

5-3

Weak Gap Stack

5-3 Stack

Eagle

Wide 6

Pro 4-3

Tight 6

College 4-3

Gap 8

4-3 Eagle

6-5

two defenders are left unblocked versus seven-man defensive fronts and three defenders are not blocked versus eight-man fronts. The following are some possible adjustments that can be made to compensate for this problem:

1. To assure maximum protection versus a seven-man front, only three receivers may initially run pass patterns (Figure 6-2).

2. If an eligible receiver who is assigned to block finds that his defender drops off into coverage, the receiver may then run a pass pattern (Figure 6-3).

3. Versus an eight-man front, a Twins formation usually forces the defense into a seven-man front. A defense that does not reduce itself is extremely vulnerable to the pass, as previously noted in Chapter 3. The only exception to this principle is illustrated in Figure 6-4. Although not as vulnerable to the pass, this adjustment is weak versus runs and play action passes toward the tight end.

4. Versus a nonreduced eight-man front, the backside end must block and both running backs should block frontside, observing the same coaching points made in #2 (Figure 6-5).

5. Versus some nonreduced eight-man fronts, one of the running backs can be assigned the dual responsibility of blocking the attackside linebacker who rushes. If both linebackers rush, the remaining running back will be open for a quick dump-off pass. The Wide 6, Tight 6, 5-3, and 5-3 Stack are all vulnerable to this tactic (Figure 6-6).

Figure 6-2

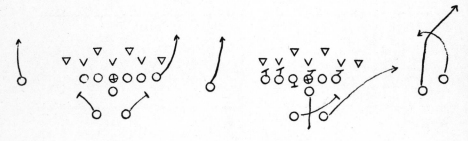

Figure 6-3

Figure 6-4

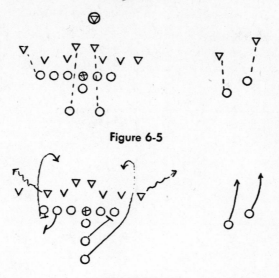

Figure 6-5

Figure 6-6

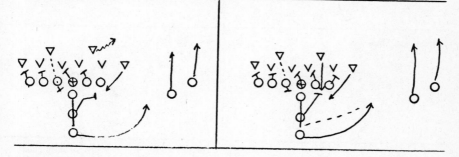

Fan Protection

Fan protection attempts to have offensive linemen block defensive linemen and running backs block linebackers. Although it is adaptable to a few eight-man fronts, we primarily use it versus seven-man fronts. Unlike Solid protection, no directional call is needed to help offensive linemen ascertain the location of their Backside Gap. The assignments for Fan protection are as follows:

AST— Block the second defender on the line of scrimmage.

ASG— Block the first defender on the line of scrimmage.

C— Check both A gaps. If there is a defender in only one of the A gaps, block him. If there are defenders in both A gaps call "Solid" (also call "Solid" if you are confronted by a Stack). If there are no defenders in the A gaps, block: On, Over.

BSG—Block the first defender on the line of scrimmage.

BST—Block the second defender on the line of scrimmage.

Note: Anytime the center calls "Solid," it means that we will not use Fan protection; instead, everyone will block Solid.

Figure 6-7 illustrates the application of Fan protection versus seven-man fronts.

Figure 6-7

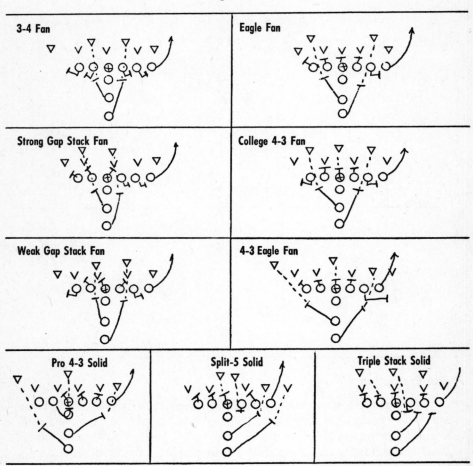

Dual Protection

Dual protection is a variation of Solid protection. The basic rule: ON, BACKSIDE GAP, HUNT is identical for both protections (a directional call "Dual Right" or "Dual Left" is also required of Dual). Dual protection differs from Solid in that offensive linemen who are assigned to Hunt an attackside linebacker have the additional assignment of looking to the outside if the linebacker they are hunting does not rush. Dual protection thus frees the running back who would normally block in the direction of the call from his protection responsibilities and enables him to run a dump-off route in the event that both attackside linebackers rush. Figure 6-8 illustrates Dual protection versus the 3-4 defense and Figure 6-9 shows it versus the Split-4.

Figure 6-8—"Dual Right" Versus 3-4

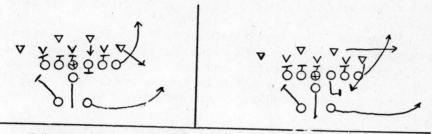

Both attackside linebackers rush; quarterback quickly dumps the ball to the running back.

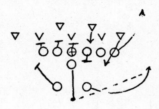

Figure 6-9—"Dual Right" Versus Split-4

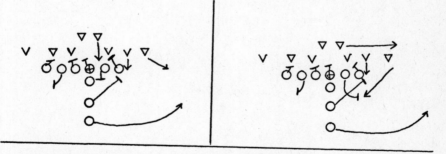

Both attackside linebackers rush, quarterback quickly dumps the ball to the running back.

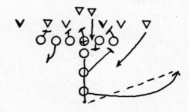

SPRINT-OUT AND SEMI-ROLL PROTECTION

Protecting a sprint-out quarterback is not much different than protecting a dropback quarterback except that less consideration need be given to backside protection, since the quarterback is rapidly moving away from this area. The application of Solid protection to the attackside and Dual protection to the backside should suffice in providing adequate time for the quarterback to unload the ball.

Versus an eight-man front, both backs must block frontside, but the back assigned to block a linebacker may run a pattern if the linebacker drops off into coverage. Versus a seven-man front, both backs can block frontside (although only one is actually needed), or the extra back may be used to run a frontside or backside route. Figure 6-10 illustrates sprint-out protection versus both seven- and eight-man fronts.

Basically, we use Solid protection to protect the semi-roll quarterback. Occasionally, we will block Solid frontside and Dual backside for patterns such as the one illustrated in Figure 6-11, but this is the exception rather than the rule.

Figure 6-10

6-10A   6-10B

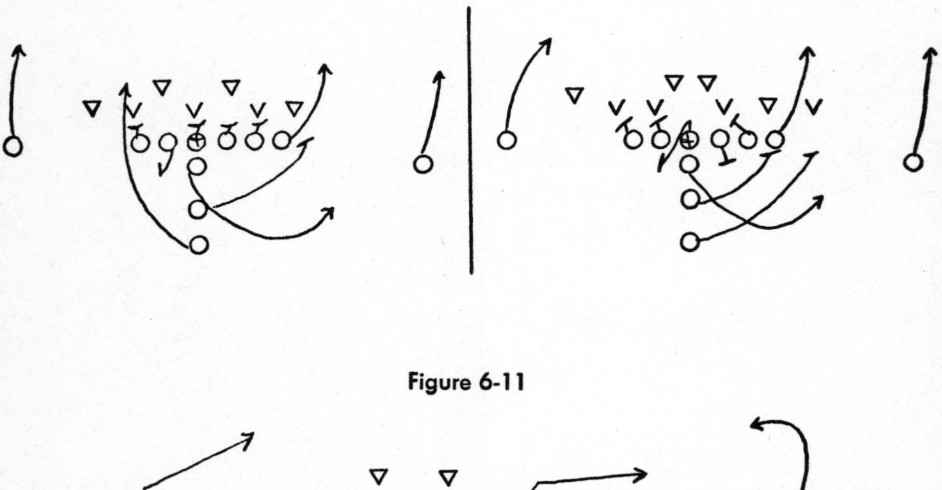

Figure 6-11

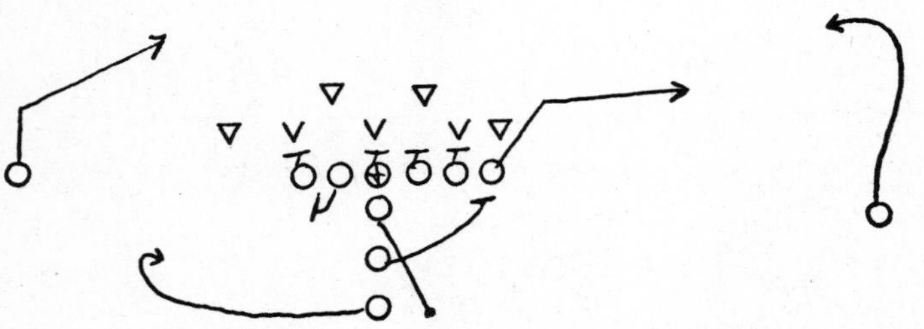

SCREEN PASSES

A well-timed, properly executed screen pass is one of football's most potent weapons. Offensive linemen have a very important role in assuring the success of a screen pass. They must be good actors and convince the defense that the play is a pass. The following are four situations in which a screen is most effective:

1. In passing situations when there is a high probability that the defense will stunt.
2. In bad weather conditions.
3. Near an opponent's goal line, where the defense is likely to put a hard rush on the quarterback.
4. When the defensive secondary and linebackers are dropping deep to stop long and medium-long passes. (The defensive line must also be rushing hard—the screen is usually ineffective if the defensive line is playing soft.)

In this section we will present five variations of the screen. These are: (1) the quick screen; (2) the long screen; (3) the short screen; (4) the middle screen and (5) the double screen. The interior line's initial blocking assignments for all five screens are identical. Their subsequent assignments vary depending upon the specific screen being employed and the particular offensive formation from which it is being thrown. The subsequent assignments for each screen will be shown in the illustrated examples. The following are the initial screen assignments for the five interior linemen:

AST: On, Over, Outside
ASG: On, Over, Reach, Stack, Hunt
 C: On, Over, Gap, Hunt
BSG: On, Over, Gap, Hunt
BST: On, Over, Gap, Hunt
BST: On, Over, Gap, Hunt

Figure 6-12 illustrates these assignments versus 14 defenses.

The Quick Screen

This play is very difficult to defend because it puts a great deal of pressure on the flank. It is most effective when a sprint draw or dropback draw is first faked. The tackle should bump his defender and release quickly to the flats. The guard should hold his block two counts before releasing to block the safety. Figure 6-13 illustrates two examples of the quick screen.

Figure 6-12—Master Call: Screen

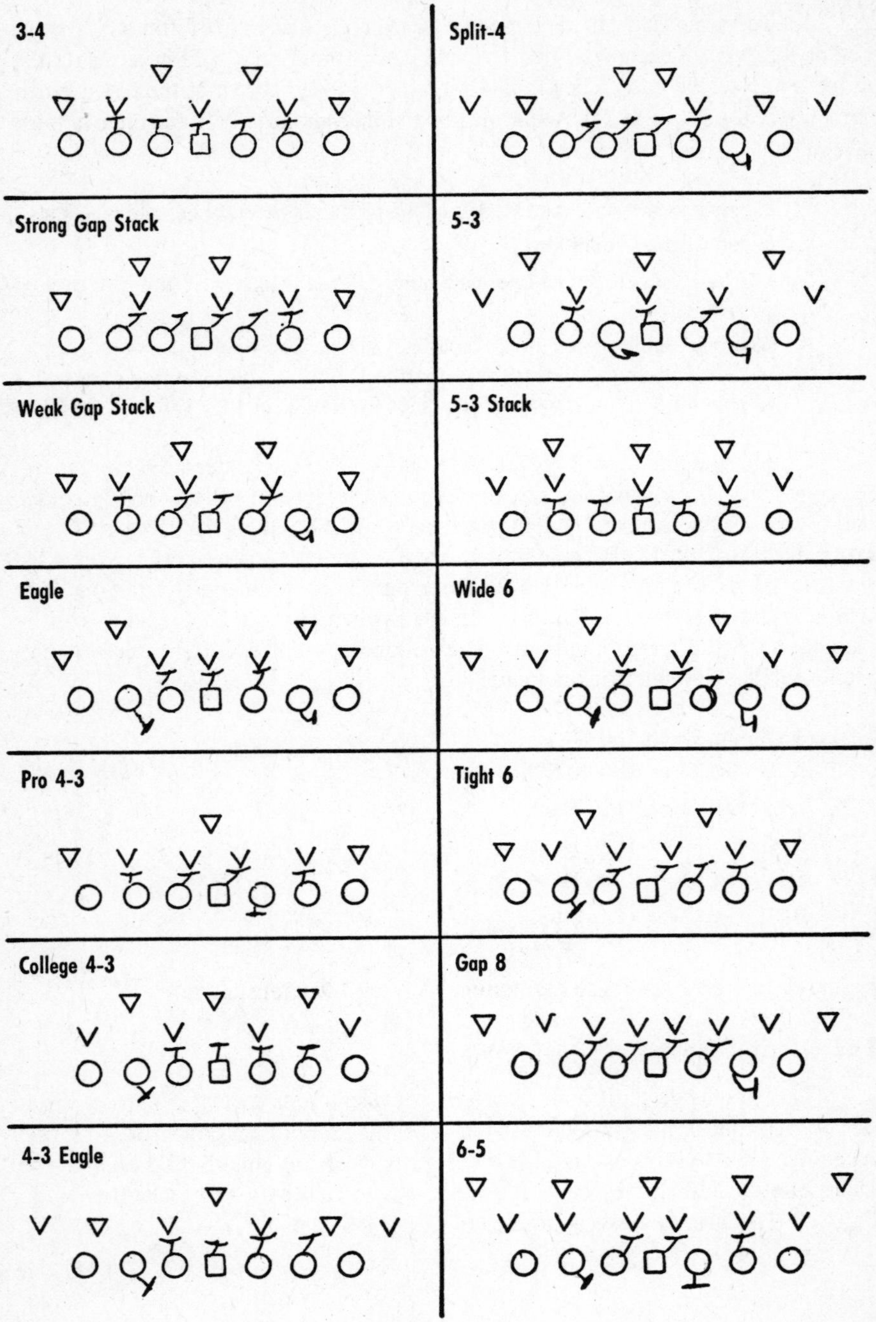

3-4

Split-4

Strong Gap Stack

5-3

Weak Gap Stack

5-3 Stack

Eagle

Wide 6

Pro 4-3

Tight 6

College 4-3

Gap 8

4-3 Eagle

6-5

Figure 6-13

3-4

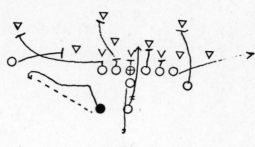

Split-4

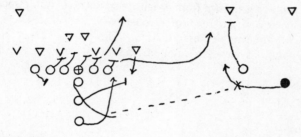

The Long Screen

This play is an ideal play action screen. Unlike other screens, the offensive linemen must convince the defense that the play is a run. This is not difficult since uncovered linemen may fire out and block linebackers anytime the ball is thrown behind the line of scrimmage. Linemen should hold their blocks for three counts before releasing to form the "wall." Figure 6-14 illustrates two examples of the long screen.

Figure 6-14

Split-4

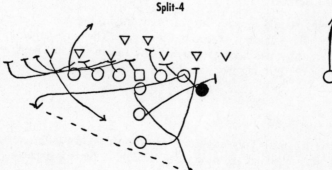

Figure 6-14 (Cont'd.)

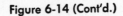

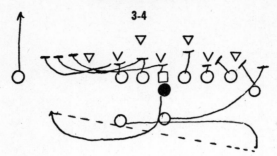

The Short Screen

The short screen is thrown from dropback action. It is very effective versus a defensive end who is alert to reading screens, because the offensive tackle stays with this man until the completion of the play. The guards and center hold their block two counts before releasing. Figure 6-15 illustrates an example of the short screen.

Figure 6-15

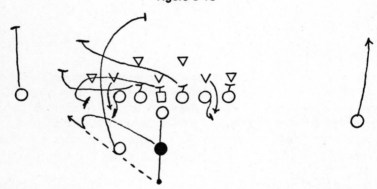

The Middle Screen

This play should also be thrown from dropback action. It is especially effective when the defense is expecting a long pass. The play should not be used against a team whose nose tackle is playing soft. Linemen should hold their block two counts before forming the wall. Figure 6-16 illustrates an example of the middle screen.

The Double Screen

This is the last of the dropback screens. It is very effective when the offense has already shown the short screen and the defense is expecting a repeat performance. Backside linemen should release after two counts, and attackside linemen should wait until three counts before releasing. Figure 6-17 illustrates an example of the double screen.

Figure 6-16

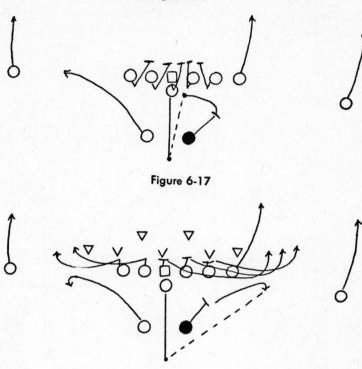

Figure 6-17

DRAWS

A draw is most effective when the linebackers are dropping off quickly to stop the pass. It is also a good play when the nose tackle is playing soft to stop the screen. Since the blitz can prove to be a menace to the draw, it is important that the offense utilize a "hot" receiver so that the quarterback can dump the ball off if the linebackers stunt. Like the screen, offensive linemen must be good actors and convince the defense that the play is a pass. Figure 6-18 illustrates four variations of the draw. Below each diagram are suggested master calls that could be used to block each play.

The Sprint Draw

Special mention should be made of the sprint draw. It is one of the finest plays in football. It is a three-dimensional play that threatens not only the off-tackle hole, but the flank and the air as well. Slice, Bend, Rip and Solid are four master calls that can be used to block the play. The main problem with these master calls, however, is that the center is assigned to block the nose tackle one-on-one versus the 3-4 defense, and, since he does not have an angle or leverage advantage, there is a high probability that a good nose tackle will stop the play with a high level of consistency. In an attempt to resolve this problem, we block the Sprint Draw in the following manner (Figure 6-19):

Figure 6-18

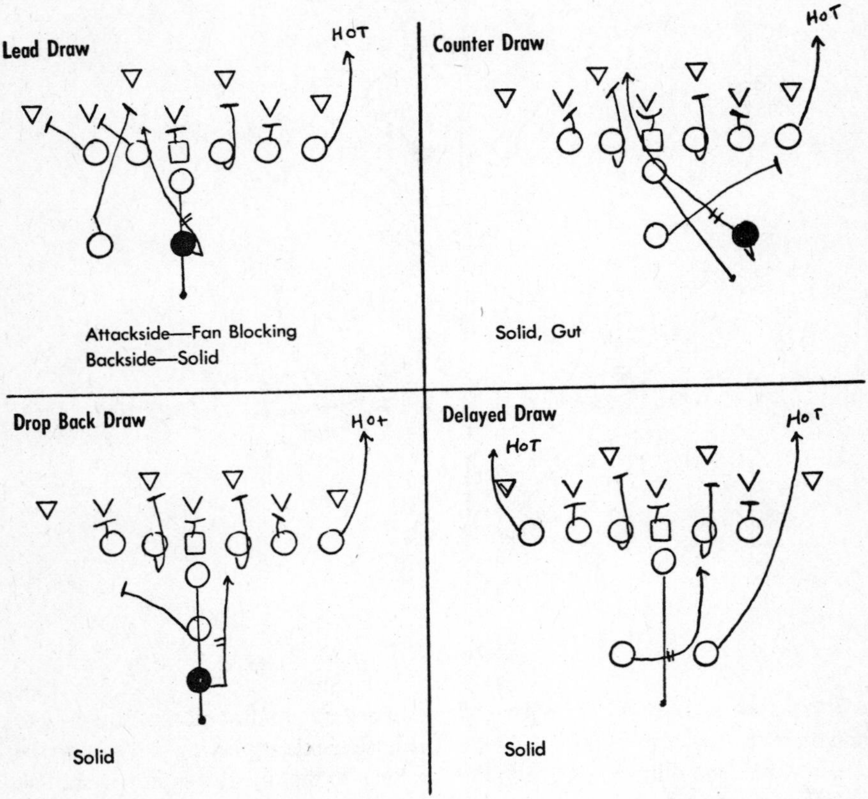
Lead Draw
HOT
Attackside—Fan Blocking
Backside—Solid
Counter Draw
HOT
Solid, Gut
Drop Back Draw
Hot
Solid
Delayed Draw
HOT
Hot
Solid

Figure 6-19

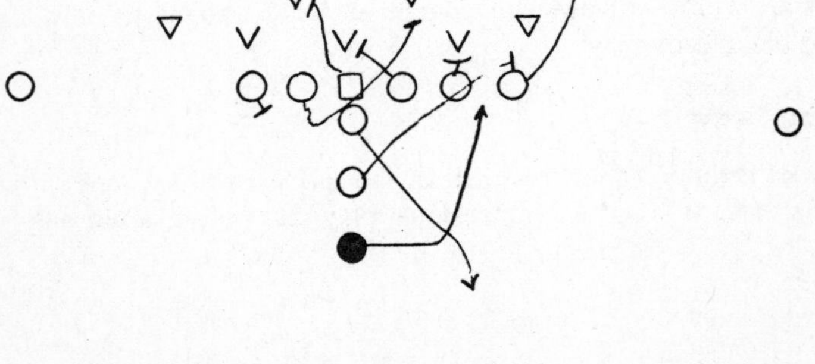

The blocking rules for the sprint draw are as follows:

ASE: Release outside and read the inside LB. If he stunts, you are the hot receiver. If he drops off into coverage, block downfield.

AST: Rule. Use pass blocking techniques and take the defender where he wants to go.

ASG: Stack, Inside, Linebacker (Curl Versus Split-4).

C: On Versus Stack, Otherwise Away.

BSG: Show pass and then pull around and block either the attackside or backside LB—whichever one is there.

BST: Rule. Use pass protection techniques.

BSE: Downfield.

Figure 6-20 illustrates Spring Draw assignments.

Figure 6-20

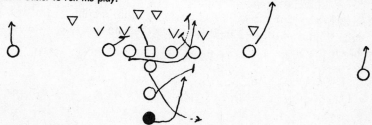

Note: Versus the Split-4, the Wide 6, etc. the tight end should flex causing the defense to adjust. This makes it easier to run the play.

PLAY ACTION PASSES

Every great offense is constructed in such a manner that running plays are organized into sequential patterns and intricately interwoven with corresponding play action passes. The success of a play action pass is primarily dependent upon an offensive team's ability to convince the defense that the play is a run. There is a difference of opinion among some coaches as to the best way of blocking a play action pass. A number of coaches believe that play action passes should be blocked in the same exact manner as the running plays that mothered them. Others feel that maximum protection should be afforded the quarterback. I personally feel that versus a reading defense, most play action passes can be blocked pretty much in the same way as their corresponding running plays, but versus stunting, gap control defenses the quarterback must be given maximum protection.

Teams that operate out of the pro formation frequently experience difficulty protecting their quarterback whenever they attempt to throw a play action pass after faking a running play in the direction of their Y end. The reason for this is because they are outnumbered toward the weak side of their formation. In an attempt to resolve this problem, I would like to introduce another protection scheme which I call Slide. Slide protection is only effective versus a seven-man front, but teams that feature the pro set should be able to force their opponents into a seven-man front or else re-evaluate the soundness of their philosophy.

The following are the rule assignments for Slide protection:

AST: On, Inside, Hunt
ASG: Inside, On, Hunt
  C: Away
BSG: Outside, Hunt
BST: Outside

Figure 6-21 illustrates Slide versus ten popular seven-man fronts.

The circled defenders in Figure 6-21 are the ones that must be blocked by the two backs faking the run. Figure 6-22 illustrates a typical pass that could be used with Slide protection.

Although space does not permit me to illustrate and explain a play action pass for every run master call presented in Chapters 2 through 4, I would like to show a dozen play action passes that could be used in conjunction with these master calls (Figures 6-23–6-34). Below each diagram is a brief explanation of how to block the play.

Figure 6-21

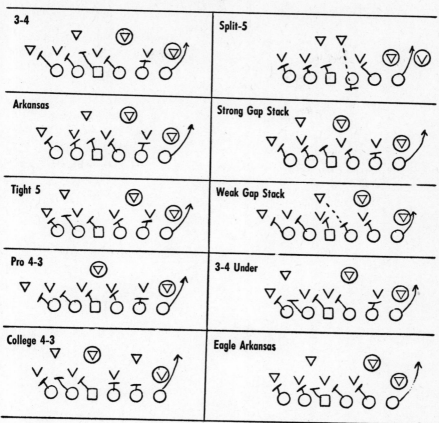

Figure 6-22

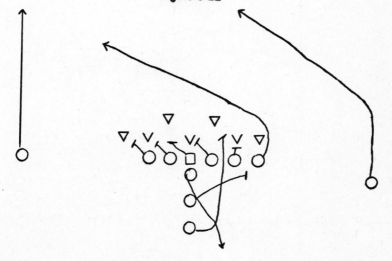

Figure 6-23

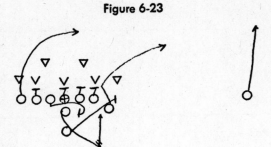

Solid protection attackside, Dual protection backside. *Note:* the curl technique by the backside guard gives the initial impression that the play is a Power.

Figure 6-24

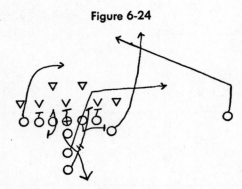

Rip blocking rules attackside, Dual protection backside. Play initially looks like a Rip or Iso.

Figure 6-25

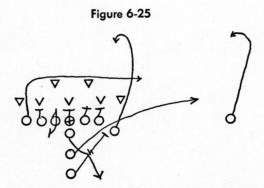

Solid protection attackside, Dual protection backside. Play initially looks like a Quick.

Figure 6-26

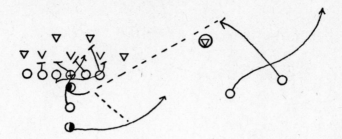

Trap option pass using trap option rules. QB keys the safety and passes if he supports the run, or runs the option if he hangs in the flats.

Figure 6-27

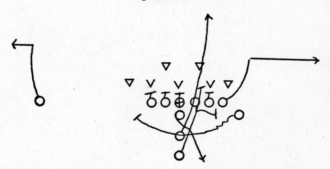

Solid protection for everyone but the attackside guard, who pulls and blocks outside.

Figure 6-28

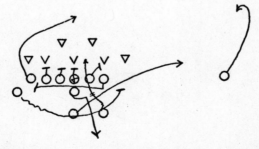

Solid protection backside and protection as diagrammed attackside. Initial impression is that the play is a tackle trap.

Figure 6-29

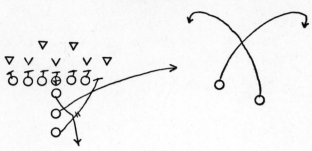

Solid protection both attackside and backside. Good pass to be used in conjunction with the quick screen.

Figure 6-30

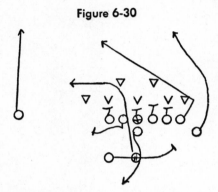

Solid protection for everyone except the attackside guard. Gives the initial impression that the play is a Gut.

Figure 6-31

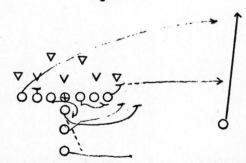

Sweep rules attackside, Dual protection backside. Note curl technique by backside guard.

Figure 6-32

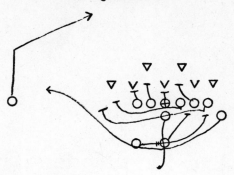

Solid protection attackside, T-Trap blocking backside.

Figure 6-33

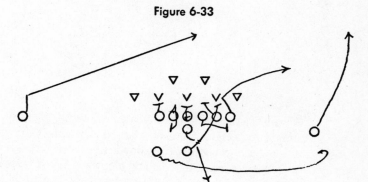

Slant blocking attackside, Dual protection backside.

Figure 6-34

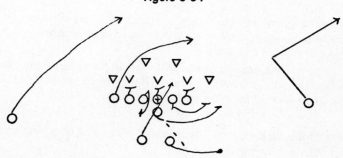

Quick pitch blocking attackside, Dual protection backside.

7

Attacking Modern Defenses Through the Effective Use of Offensive Formations

A subject that is frequently overlooked by many football coaches is that of formation selection. Some coaches take the matter for granted and mistakenly assume that it is impossible to err in the selection process. Others choose formations in the same manner that they do clothes—they select what is popular, or in vogue. Many coaches select formations because: "that's what last year's National Champion did," or because a smooth-talking speaker at last year's clinic "made it sound awfully good."

In reality, formation selection is a vital issue for two very important reasons. These are:

1. One of the primary keys to winning football is the proper utilization of talent. It is impossible to efficiently utilize talent without aligning personnel in positions that will enhance their abilities.
2. Formations constitute a manipulative device that forces the defense into adjustments. If wrong decisions are made and the defense adjusts improperly, the offense is afforded an additional means of attack.

The purpose of this chapter is to discuss some of the key considerations in the selection of offensive formations.

TO SPLIT AN END OR NOT TO SPLIT AN END?

Most teams split at least one end. The advantages of splitting an end can be great. Not only does the split end spread the defensive secondary, but there is a high probability that if he is isolated in a one-on-one situation with a defensive back, that he will be able to outmaneuver the defender a large percentage of the time. Furthermore, if the split end is truly a great athlete, there is a good possibility that the defense may double-cover him and thus weaken themselves in their ability to cover other receivers and/or stop the running game.

Teams that are truly committed to throwing the ball, must out of necessity split at least one end. Teams not so committed, either as a result of philosophy or lack of talent, should carefully analyze whether or not they will be able to effectively compensate for the gap that they will be conceding to the defense. One must keep in mind that the utilization of a split end leaves the defense with only seven gaps to defend—this enables all defenses, even seven-man fronts, to overshift their alignment and thus outnumber the offense on both sides of the center (Figure 7-1).

Figure 7-1

Versus two tight ends, the defense is forced to defend eight gaps with seven defenders.

Versus only one tight end, the defense is afforded the luxury of being able to defend seven gaps with seven defenders. They can thus overshift their alignment.

PRESSURING THE DEFENSE WITH LARGE LINE SPLITS

When the offense assumes large line splits, the defense is forced to defend more territory. As a result of this predicament, the defense has two options: (1) they can move out with offensive linemen, and as a result possibly leave themselves vulnerable to inside plays, or (2) they can align or stunt themselves into the gaps and thus give offensive linemen better blocking angles for outside plays.

The primary consideration in deciding on whether or not to assume large line splits should, of course, be the quickness of the offensive line. "Jake" Gaither, the former legendary great coach at Florida A & M, proved that quick linemen can assume line splits as large as 4 1/2 feet and adequately protect the gaps from defensive penetration. Linemen who possess average or below average quickness, however, would not be able to assume such large splits. A coach must thus assess the quickness of his personnel when considering the feasibility of large line splits.

Coaches who decide that large line splits are feasible for their particular situation, will find that there are a number of Radar master calls, that when used in conjunction with one another, will fulfill their needs. Two such master calls are Power and Inside Ice. Versus the 3-4 defense, for example, the defense will be vulnerable to the Power if the defensive end moves into the B gap, when the offensive tackle assumes a large line split. They would conversely be vulnerable to the Inside Ice when the defensive end doesn't move into the B gap (Figure 7-2). The same principles hold true versus the Split-4 defense, when the tight end assumes a large split (Figure 7-3).

Figure 7-2

7-2A—Poor adjustment to Inside Ice   7-2B—Poor adjustment to Power

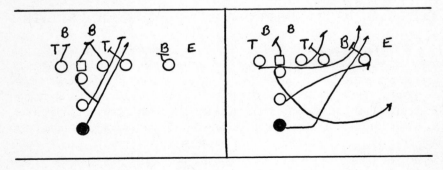

Figure 7-3

7-3A—Poor adjustment to Outside Ice   7-3B—Poor adjustment to Power

UTILIZING A SLOTBACK OR A WINGBACK

The difference between a slotback and a wingback is that a slotback plays outside of an offensive tackle; whereas, a wingback plays outside of the tight end (Figure 7-4).

Figure 7-4

Normal Slotback	Tight Slotback	Tight Wingback
⊕○○ ○ ○	⊕○○ ○ ○	⊕○○○ ○

There are four advantages of employing a normal slotback. These are:

1. The slotback forces the defense to defend the eighth gap—the one that was conceded by the utilization of the split end.
2. The slotback poses a more meaningful counter-threat than does a tight end.
3. The slotback can be sent into motion for the following reasons:
   a. To create a pro formation (Figure 7-5A).
   b. To create a twins formation (Figure 7-5B).
   c. To cause needless movement in the secondary (Figure 7-5C).
   d. To act as a lead blocker (Figure 7-5 D & E).
   e. To become a ball carrier (Figure 7-5 F).
   f. To create misdirection (Figure 7-5G).
4. The slotback gives the offense all of the advantages of two tight ends, four running backs and a split end.

A tight wingback gives the offense the same motion and counter-threat advantages as did the normal slotback. Furthermore, a tight wingback forces the defense to defend eight gaps when used in conjunction with a split end and nine gaps when used with two tight ends. Also, a tight wingback places the offense in a serious adjustment dilemma. If the defense plays their outside linebacker inside of the wingback, he becomes vulnerable to the crack-back block (Figure 7-6A). On the other hand, if the outside linebacker plays outside of the wingback, the entire defense becomes vulnerable to the off-tackle play (Figure 7-6B).

It should also be noted that whenever the outside linebacker plays inside of the wingback, he is vulnerable to a serious assignment conflict dilemma. If he honors the influence block of the wingback and fights outside pressure, he becomes assailable to the off-tackle play (Figure 7-7A). On the other hand, if he ignores the influence block, he becomes susceptible to the crack-back block (Figure 7-7B).

Figure 7-5

7-5A—Motion into a Pro Formation

7-5B—Motion into a Twins Formation

7-5C—False Motion

7-5D—The slotback as a lead blocker

7-5E—The slotback as a lead blocker

7-5F—The slotback as a ball carrier

7-5G—Misdirection Motion

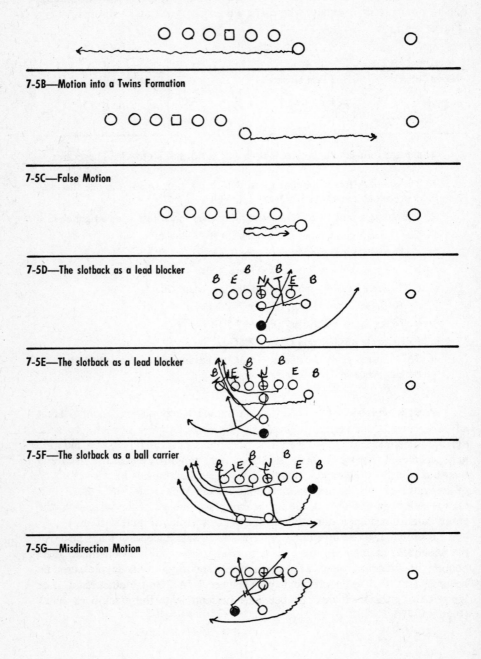

Figure 7-6

7-6A

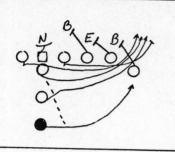

7-6B

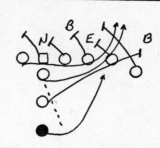

Figure 7-7

7-7A

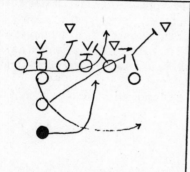

7-7B

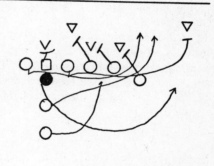

By reacting to the influence of the wingback, the OLB is vulnerable to the off-tackle play.

By not reacting to the wingback, the OLB is vulnerable to the outside.

The tight slotback poses all of the same problems to the offense that the tight wingback does. The reason that some teams employ a tight slotback rather than a tight wingback is because of the difficulty that a wingback might experience attempting to block an outside linebacker. Obviously, because the tight end is bigger than the wingback, he is more suited to block an outside linebacker. It should also be noted that most teams that employ a tight slotback will utilize the Sweep master call rather than the Stampede master call to engineer their outside running plays (Figure 7-8).

Figure 7-8

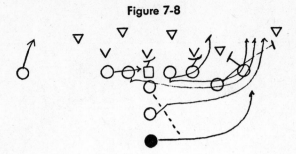

FACTORS TO CONSIDER IN THE SELECTION OF A BACKFIELD SET

The decisions that one makes regarding the selection of a backfield set(s) is vital. The prime consideration should, of course, be the talents of available personnel. Rather than settling on one specific backfield set, some coaches prefer to employ multiple sets. This enables them to be more versatile in their attack. If multiple sets are employed, however, a coach must be careful not to allow his offense to become predictable. The best way to insure against predictability is to constantly scout your own offense, checking to make sure that you don't always do the same things from the same backfield sets. Teams that do many things from each backfield set are the least predictable.

The following are factors that should be considered in the selection of a backfield set:

I Backs (Fig. 7-9)

1. Predominately a tailback orientated set, which enables the best running back (the tailback) to quickly hit every hole, utilizing the benefits of a lead blocker.
2. A balanced set that enables the offense to attack all sectors of the defense with equal effectiveness.
3. Unless a slotback or wingback is utilized, the offense is limited in its counter game.
4. Unless the option, or gut series, are used (these two series will be discussed in detail in Chapter 8), the offense limits its ability to effectively utilize the fullback.
5. Unless slotback or wingback motion is employed, it is difficult to provide the fullback with a lead blocker. (Refer to Figure 6-5D.)

Figure 7-9

○ ○ ○ ▢ ○ ○ ○
○
○
○

"T" Backs (Fig. 7-10)

1. Excellent set to fully utilize the abilities of a good fullback.
2. Good formation for counter plays.
3. Excellent set to involve the halfback in the passing game.
4. If the halfback is used to run sweeps and off-tackle plays (toward the fullback), he must possess above-average speed.
5. The running game is probably more effective toward the side of the formation to which the halfback is aligned.
6. The halfback can be used as an influence blocker, or lead blocker, in a similar fashion previously described for the wingback.
7. The ball carrying abilities of the halfback can be best utilized with dives, quick pitches, counters (and sweeps and off-tackle plays), providing he possesses adequate speed.

Figure 7-10

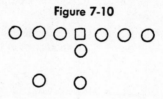

Wide Split Backs (Fig. 7-11)

1. Excellent formation to involve both running backs in the passing game.
2. Unless a wingback or slotback is used, the formation is extremely limited in its counter ability.
3. Quick hitting plays, such as dives, traps and quick pitches, are probably the best running plays.
4. In order to effectively use sweeps and off-tackle plays, the running backs must be exceptionally quick.
5. This is one of the most difficult sets from which to develop a sequential run offense.

Figure 7-11

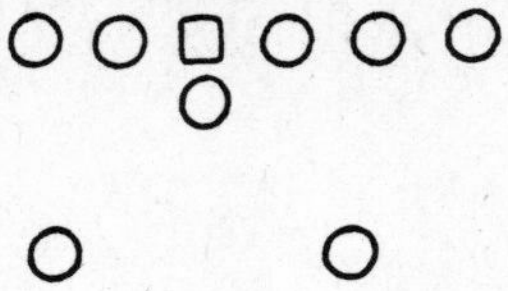

O O ▢ O O O
O

O   O

Tight Split Backs (Fig. 7-12)

1. Great formation for the veer offense.
2. Possesses most of the advantages and disadvantages of both the I and wide split backs.

Figure 7-12

O O ▢ O O O
O

O   O

Full House Sets (Fig. 7-13)

1. Good passing formations, when used in conjunction with play action passes. None of the four formations are suitable to the dropback game, however, unless one of the running backs is sent into motion.
2. All four formations combine both the strengths and weaknesses of other formations. (Example: the Power I is a combination of both the I- and T-backs.)

Figure 7-13

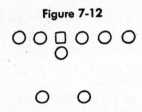

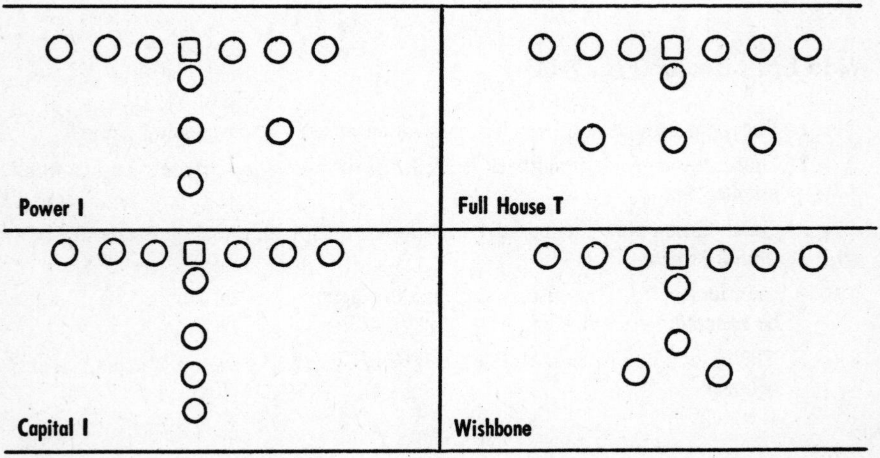

Power I	Full House T
Capital I	Wishbone

Single Back Set (Fig. 7-14)

1. Great passing set.

2. Must be used in conjunction with slotbacks and/or wingbacks, and motion, in order to establish sequence in the running game.

3. The only way that an effective running game can be established without using slotback or wingback motion is to force the defense to reduce its front to five or six defenders, by achieving a high degree of productivity with the pass, or by being gifted with a running back of the calibre of John Riggins.

Figure 7-14

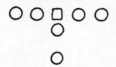

CADENCE, SHIFTS, MOTION AND "AWSONIMITY"

As a conclusion to this chapter, I would like to introduce you to a new word. The word is "awsonimity." You won't find the word in the dictionary, because I made it up. The reason that I had to make it up is because Webster forgot to. Awsonimity describes a very important time line that exists in the life of every defensive football player. This time line begins when an offensive team breaks the huddle and ends when they snap the ball.

An offensive team has total control over awsonimity. The defense has absolutely no control. An offensive team can make awsonimity a very painless, uncomplicated affair for the defense, or they can make it very complex and unpleasant. Time is a vital element during awsonimity. The longer the awsonimity, the more time a defensive player has to recognize the formation, recall tendencies, etc. The shorter the awsonimity, the less time the defender has to do these things.

Figures 7-15 and 7-16 illustrate and explain the activities of two different teams during awsonimity. Both teams utilize equal time durations during awsonimity. The A Team, however, causes the defense to make many more adjustments and go through a much more complex thought pattern. Also, as a result of their activities, the A Team prevents the defense from stemming and jumping around, in an attempt to confuse offensive linemen. The defense is too involved with their own adjustment problems to even consider causing havoc. They are forced to scramble for their lives.

The moral of this discussion is as follows:

1. If you choose to shift your offense, do it quickly and in a manner that will present *real* problems to the defense. Don't loll around and involve yourself in token shifts that are near meaningless to defense.

2. Use your cadence to create your own tempo. The longer you "talk" at the line, the more time you give the defense to think, stem, and jump around.

3. Audibles are fine, but if the defense is really giving you pre-snap reads, they don't know what they are doing and you will probably beat them anyway. Besides, most pre-snap reads are defensive attempts to camouflage post-snap activites.

4. If motion is employed, do it as quickly as possible—*sprint*! Don't give the defense ample time to adjust.

5. Use awsonimity to your advantage, not to the advantage of the defense.

Figure 7-15—"The A Team"

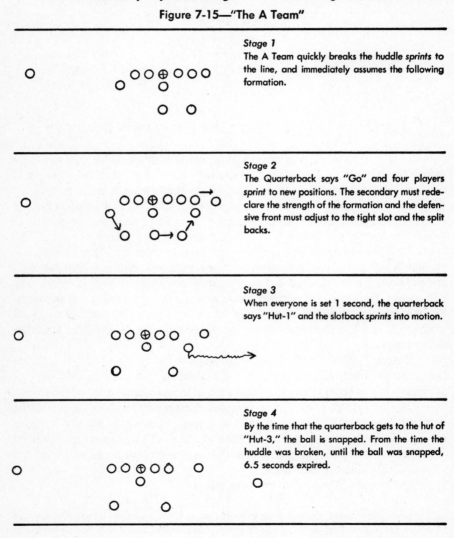

Stage 1
The A Team quickly breaks the huddle *sprints* to the line, and immediately assumes the following formation.

Stage 2
The Quarterback says "Go" and four players *sprint* to new positions. The secondary must redeclare the strength of the formation and the defensive front must adjust to the tight slot and the split backs.

Stage 3
When everyone is set 1 second, the quarterback says "Hut-1" and the slotback *sprints* into motion.

Stage 4
By the time that the quarterback gets to the hut of "Hut-3," the ball is snapped. From the time the huddle was broken, until the ball was snapped, 6.5 seconds expired.

Figure 7-16—"The B Team"

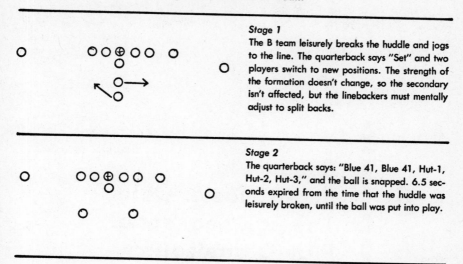

Stage 1

The B team leisurely breaks the huddle and jogs to the line. The quarterback says "Set" and two players switch to new positions. The strength of the formation doesn't change, so the secondary isn't affected, but the linebackers must mentally adjust to split backs.

Stage 2

The quarterback says: "Blue 41, Blue 41, Hut-1, Hut-2, Hut-3," and the ball is snapped. 6.5 seconds expired from the time that the huddle was leisurely broken, until the ball was put into play.

8 Enhancing Radar Master Calls Through Sequential Play Organization

The difference between an offense and a "bunch of plays" is sequence. Sequence, as it applies to football, can be defined as the grouping of similar backfield actions and blocking patterns for the purpose of:

1. Attacking the defense over a broad front. A sequential series will attack all sectors of the defense—the inside sector, the off-tackle hole, the perimeter and the secondary.
2. Causing initial uncertainty in the minds of defensive players. What at first appears to be an off-tackle play, could end up being a sweep, a counter, a reverse or a pass. Uncertainty slows defensive reaction and pursuit.
3. Placing defenders in an assignment conflict dilemma. This destroys keys and defensive confidence.

When one examines the most explosive offenses, the winningest coaches and the most consistently successful programs of the past three or four decades, it soon becomes apparent that offensive ascendancy and sequential football are synonymous. The following examples are some of the greatest offensive systems in the annals of modern football, and all were built by men who firmly believed in the merits of sequential football:

— Bud Wilkenson's powerful Split-T
— Dave Nelson and H.R. "Tubby" Raymond's Delaware Wing-T
— Jake Gaither's devastating Split-Line T
— Vince Lombardi's great Green Bay offense
— Eddie Robinson's Grambling Wing-T
— Ara Parseghians' explosive Multiple I-Wing-T
— The great wishbone teams of Oklahoma, Texas and Alabama
— Woody Hayes' fabulous Ohio State power offense
— Bill Yeoman's Houston Veer
— The great I teams of USC and Penn State

The list could go on and on, but there is no need for that. It is obvious that sequential football is winning football. Sequential play organization is an equalizer that enables inferior offensive personnel to consistently defeat superior defensive opponents by preventing defenders from "teeing off," or "winding up." The remainder of this chapter will illustrate and explain five sequential series that I have used throughout the years. I am indebted to the many fine coaches who have shared their ideas and wisdom with me, thus enabling me to formulate these series.

THE POWER SERIES

Figure 8-1

Power

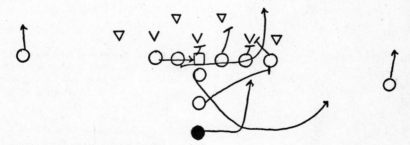

This is the base play of the series. The Power master call is the suggested method of engineering this backfield action. Quick Y and Punch are also effective master calls versus stunting defenses. Proper utilization of line splits and/or a tight wingback can greatly enhance the play.

Figure 8-1 (Cont'd.)

The Quarterback Keep

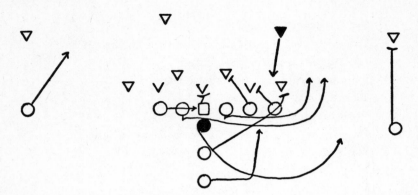

The quarterback keep is the outside counterpart of the power. The strong safety's reaction to the power is a coach's key to calling the quarterback keep. Whenever the strong safety begins to react too quickly to the power, the quarterback keep will be the next logical play selection. There are at least three ways in which this play can be blocked. These are:

1. The illustrated example—The Stampede master call, utilizing the fullback to block the outside linebacker.
2. The Stampede master call used in conjunction with a tight wingback (the wingback blocks the outside linebacker and the fullback leads).
3. Using the same exact rules as the power.

T-Trap

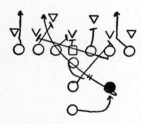

The T-Trap is a counter that takes advantage of defenses that react too quickly to stop the power. Although its blocking pattern does not complement the power master scheme, its backfield action does.

The Fullback Counter

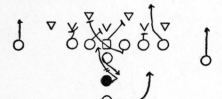

The fullback counter serves as a quick-hitting misdirection play, whose backfield action complements that of the power. The following are ways in which the play can be blocked:

1. Trap master call.
2. Gut master call.
3. Quick Y master call (X combo call between the BSG & C versus the College 4-3 and 4-3 Eagle defenses, or a X combo call versus the BSG and BST versus the Split-4 defense).

Figure 8-1 (Cont'd.)

The Sprint Draw

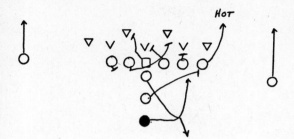

The Sprint Draw is the Power series alternative to the pass in long yardage situations.

The Power Screen

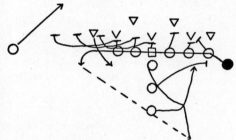

The Power Screen is a counter-type pass that takes advantage of quick-pursuing defenses, or stunting defenses that feature man-to-man coverage.

The Power Delay Pass

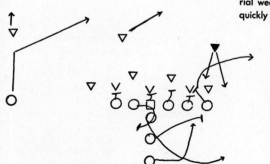

The Power Delay pass serves as an effective aerial weapon against secondaries that react too quickly to the Power, or the quarterback keep.

Figure 8-1 (Cont'd.)

The Power Quick Screen

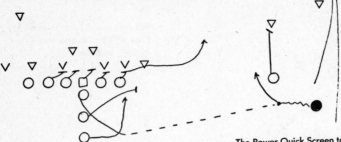

The Power Quick Screen takes advantage of poor secondary adjustments to a twins formation.

The Tackle Trap Pass

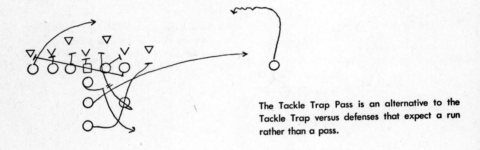

The Tackle Trap Pass is an alternative to the Tackle Trap versus defenses that expect a run rather than a pass.

THE GUT SERIES

Figure 8-2

The Gut Stampede

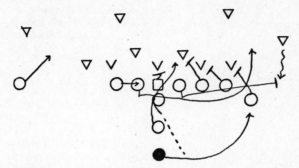

The Gut Stampede is the base play of the series. The play is most effective when it is run toward a tight wingback. The play itself is not very impressive and probably would not be very effective if it were not for the complementary plays in the series that place defenders in assignment conflict dilemmas. *Note:* If the outside linebacker plays outside of the wingback, the blast should be called rather than the stampede.

The 30 Trap

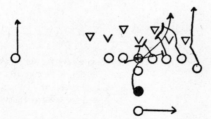

The fullback (30) trap, is the lead-off play of the series. Although the play can also be used with a Quick or Gut master call, the Trap master call does the best job of enhancing the entire series. The Trap places the defensive end in an assignment conflict. If he closes hard with the offensive tackle and plays the trap, he becomes vulnerable to either the blast or the stampede. On the other hand, if he reacts outside when the end blocks down, he is vulnerable to the trap.

Figure 8-2 (Cont'd.)

The Blast

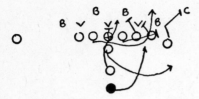

The Blast puts the outside linebacker in an assignment conflict. If he closes hard with the tight end and protects the off-tackle hole, he is vulnerable to the stampede. If he doesn't, he is vulnerable to the blast.

The Trap Option

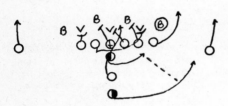

The trap option places the defensive end in an assignment conflict. If he plays the trap, the option becomes an effective play. If he doesn't play the trap, he becomes vulnerable to it.

The Trap Option Pass

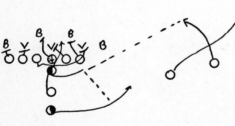

This pass places the strong safety in an assignment conflict. If he supports the run, he leaves himself vulnerable to the pass. If he plays pass, the option becomes an effective play.

The 20 Trap

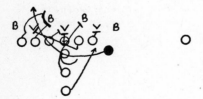

The slotback (20) trap, is the counter play for the gut series. This is the fastest hitting, most effective trap play that I have ever coached.

Figure 8-2 (Cont'd.)

The Double Dive—Option Package

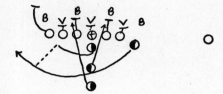

Using a Quick master call a devastating package can be created that enhances gut backfield action.

The Bootleg Pass

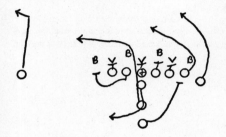

This pass is effective when the defense allows the fullback to release freely through the line. It places the outside linebacker in a dilemma. If he contains the quarterback, the fullback should be open. If he covers the fullback, he is vulnerable to the quarterback bootleg.

THE SLANT SERIES

Figure 8-3

Slant

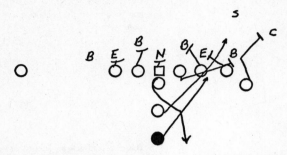

This series should be used rather than the Power series when the quarterback is not a good runner. The slant is the lead-off play of the series. The play can also be blocked with Quick, Quick Y, Bend, Slice and Rip master calls.

The Wide Slant

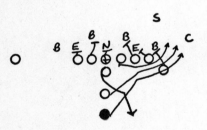

The Wide Slant is the outside counterpart of the slant. The reason that modified slant rules are used instead of Stampede rules is because it is not possible for the backside guard to pull and lead the tailback.

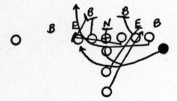

The Y-Trap is a power counter that provides the wingback with a lead blocker. It is extremely effective versus quick-pursuing defenses and defenses that slant, or overshift their alignment toward the wingback.

Figure 8-3 (Cont'd.)

Reverse

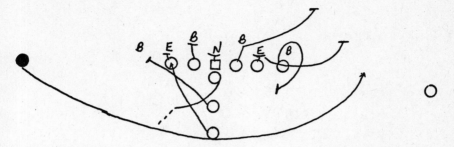

The reverse is a special surprise play that should be used sparingly. It requires a quick, nifty running split end and an over-pursuing defense to be successful.

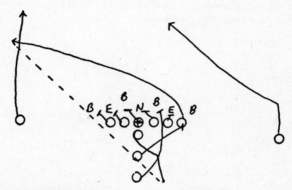

This pass challenges the deep backside third of a rotating zone secondary.

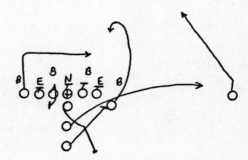

This pass can be used to attack the frontside hook zone, or man-man coverage.

THE ISO SERIES

Figure 8-4

The Inside Ice and Iso Option

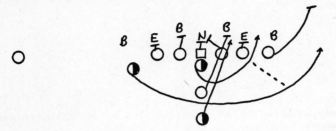

Those two plays are an explosive duo that attack all sectors of the defense—the inside sector (Inside Ice), the off-tackle hole (Quarterback Keep) and the outside sector (Pitch).

The Tailback Counter

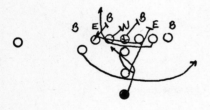

The tailback counter with either Squeeze or Trap blocking provides the offense with a powerful counter-play.

Off-Tackle Variations

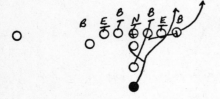

Rip, Bend, Slice, Slant or Quick blocking provides the offense with an effective means of attacking the off-tackle hole, utilizing backfield action that complements the Inside Ice.

Figure 8-4 (Cont'd.)

Enhancing the Series with Wingback Motion

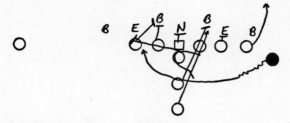

Wingback motion can be used to create misdirection. If the ball is given to the wingback (as shown), Squeeze or Trap blocking can be used. If the ball is given to the tailback, the Inside Ice, or an off-tackle variation can be employed.

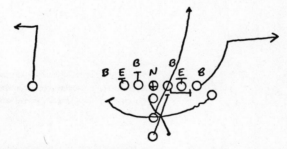

This misdirection play action pass is particularly effective versus man-man coverage.

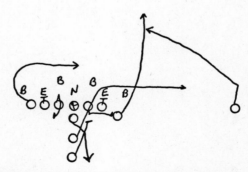

This is an excellent play action pass that can be used to attack the deep middle third of the secondary, or man-man coverage.

THE OPTION SERIES

The Dive Option

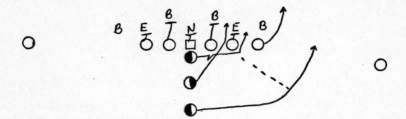

The Dive Option is one of the most magnificent plays ever devised. The play challenges all sectors of the defense.

Inside Veer

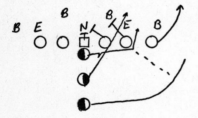

This play is particularly effective when the defense is successfully playing the defensive end on the quarterback and the outside linebacker on the pitch.

Outside Veer

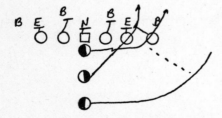

This is a great play that puts tremendous pressure on the outside linebacker.

Figure 8-5 (Cont'd.)

Slant

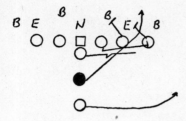

The Slant can force the outside linebacker to tackle the fullback on the outside veer.

Slotback Counter

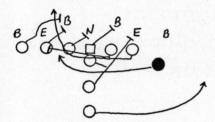

The slotback counter, with Squeeze blocking, provides the series with a quick-hitting, powerful counter-play.

Reverse

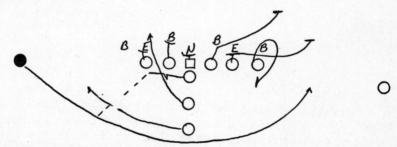

This play attacks a quick-pursuing defense and utilizes the running abilities of the split end.

Option Pass

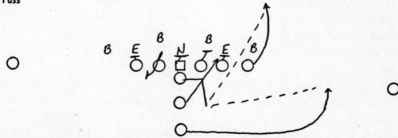

This play puts considerable pressure on the defender responsible for the pitch.

How to Integrate Radar Assignments with Sound Blocking Fundamentals

SAFETY FIRST!

Although tackling causes more fatalities and catastrophic injuries than any other football activity, blocking has claimed more than its share of victims. Most of the players who sustain serious blocking injuries receive head or neck injuries. High School players are particularly vulnerable to head and neck injuries because they have immature bone, ligamentous and cartilaginous structures, and the muscular strength of their necks' is weak. As professional educators, football coaches have a very serious obligation to do everything and anything that they possibly can to help eliminate this menacing problem. Two ways that offensive line coaches might assist in this endeavor are:

1. Don't teach butt blocking! Butt blocking is forbidden by the rules, it is unsafe and it has been condemned by the American Football Coaches Association. Furthermore, if one of your players is seriously injured while attempting to butt block an opponent, there is a good likelihood that you and/or your school

district will be sued. A recent court decision in Seattle, Washington awarded over $6 million to a football player who sustained a catastrophic neck injury while attempting to spear tackle an opponent. The defendants were found liable *not* because the coaching staff taught spear tackling, but rather because they did not: (1) drill the player in such a way that it would remove any instinctive urge to spear tackle; (2) read players the rule that forbids spear tackling; (3) hand out written material and/or use visual aids that warn both the player and his parents of the dangers associated with spear tackling. This is a landmark decision with a very powerful message to our profession. If we do not heed this message, the future of football may be in serious jeopardy.

2. Insist that your players are involved in a mandatory year-round neck strengthening program. By the very nature of the sport, some head-on collisions may be unavoidable. This is especially true of an activity such as blocking. To prepare players for these occasions, a coach must insist that all of his players develop a powerful neck musculature.

STANCE, START AND ALIGNMENT

Stance—Guards, Tackles and Tight End

1. A three-point stance is recommended. A four-point stance simply does not afford enough mobility to accommodate the needs of the Radar system.

2. Not all players will assume identical stances. Differences in body builds, prior habits, etc., will account for the variance. A player's stance should be comfortable for him, fundamentally sound and balanced so that he has mobility in all four directions.

3. Consistency is a vital factor. A player should line up the same way every time. His stance cannot become a defensive key.

4. The feet should be pointed straight ahead and they should be spread no farther than shoulder width. A good coaching point is to tell a player to align his feet directly under his armpits.

5. Guards should strive to keep their feet parallel. Tackles and Tight Ends may stagger one foot, but this stagger should be no greater than toe-heel.

6. The heels should be off the ground and the ankles should be locked.

7. As the player squats down, his knees should be spread so that they are in line with his toes. One of the most common mistakes of high school players is to spread their knees too wide, or else to have their knees inside of their toes. Both positions inhibit a quick, powerful takeoff.

8. When viewed from the side, the lower portion of a player's leg should be approximately perpendicular to the upper portion.

9. The hips should be elevated so that the back is parallel to the ground.

10. The shoulders must be parallel to the line of scrimmage and completely straight; neither shoulder should be lower or higher than the other.

11. The neck should be bulled, and the eyes should be looking straight ahead.

12. The down hand should be slightly in front of the head and in line with, or slightly inside of, the knee that it proceeds. The weight should be resting on the fingertips and not the knuckles.

13. High school players should rest the forearm of their up arm on the upper portion of their leg. College and Pro players will place the palm of this hand on their hips. Since the latter are allowed to use their hands in blocking, this position will allow them to ''wind up'' and thus afford them greater explosion into the defender.

14. The muscles in the upper portion of the player's legs must be coiled, tense and ready to explode him out of his stance the moment that the ball is hiked.

15. A player's weight should be equally distributed on the tripod formed by his feet and his down hand.

Stance—Center

1. There is not a great deal of difference between the center's stance and the stance of the other linemen. The remaining coaching points will note the things that differentiate the center's stance.

2. The feet may be spread slightly wider than the shoulders, but not too wide.

3. The hips should be elevated slightly higher than normal—especially if the center has a short inseam.

4. The center can also shift a greater portion of his weight forward.

5. The most difficult thing to teach the center is to hike the ball and move forward at the same time. Most young centers want to hike the ball and then move.

Start

1. The start is vital—no energy can be wasted on needless motion.

2. Linemen must come out of their stance by quickly stepping in the direction that they intend to go. Any ''false stepping'' must be eliminated.

3. It is vital that linemen stay low during their initial stage of takeoff.

4. Arm action is extremely important. The legs work only as fast as the arms. If a player learns to work his arms rapidly, his legs will follow suit. Linemen must be coached to bend their arms as tight as possible and keep them bent in this manner while they are sprinting. Also, the elbows must be kept close to the ribs and the fists pumped up and down—not swung from side to side across the chest.

5. Additional coaching points for sprinting are as follows:

    a. Relax—if you tighten up, you slow yourself down.

    b. Stay up on the balls of your feet and point your toes straight ahead.

    c. Push off the ground with maximum force.

    d. High knee action is extremely important.

    e. Maintain a good forward lean.

    f. Do not waste energy by moving your head from side to side.

Alignment

Our normal line splits are fairly standard. Our guard's split is 2 feet and everyone else's split is 3 feet. As I mentioned in Chapter 7, versus certain defenses, some players will assume larger-than-normal line splits for the purpose of: (1) creating larger running lanes, or (2) to give a lineman an angle advantage over the defense. Down at the goal line, or versus very quick stunting defenses, we may tighten our line splits.

Like many teams, we do not align our guards on the line of scrimmage. Instead, we align these players 2 feet off the line. This alignment enables the guards to pull "into the line," rather than parallel to it. It also affords the guards additional time and space to recognize stunts and execute the various techniques of their combo calls. All other linemen align on the line.

THE ONE-ON-ONE OR "DRIVE" BLOCK

Target

1. When blocking a down lineman, aim your eyes at his chin.
2. When blocking a linebacker, aim your eyes at the base of his numbers.

Approach

1. Your first step should be with the foot that is closest to the point of attack. In other words, if the play is to your right, your first step should be with your right foot.
2. As you fire out, your movements should be forward and not upward.
3. Keep your neck bulled. Do not duck your head as you approach the defender.
4. Keep your feet shoulder width apart and your toes pointing straight ahead. This will give you a good wide base which will enhance your balance and protect you from any broadside pressure techniques that your opponent might attempt to employ.

Contact (The following techniques comply with high school rules.)

1. Just prior to contact, slip your head to the side, between the defender and the point of attack.
2. Initial contact should be made with the shoulder and the forearm "flipper." Quickly explode the "flipper" into your opponent. If the "flipper" is not thrown rapidly enough, you will be giving your opponent something to grab onto.
3. Do not attempt to strike the defender with your "flipper." Try to hit an imaginary spot 1 yard behind the defender. In other words, drive through your opponent.
4. As contact is made, you must be lower than your opponent.
5. Lock your hips as you explode into the defender.
6. Maintain a good blocking surface with your "flipper" parallel to the ground and your ear tightly positioned against your opponent's hip.
7. Remember that you must not only drive the defender backwards, but you must also maintain contact with him until the play ends.

Contact (The following techniques are only permissible in college and pro football.)

1. As you explode off the line, a good "windup" with your arms is vital.
2. Initial contact is made with the heels of your hands. Drive your hands through your opponent's shoulders. It is vital that your hand contact is underneath the defender's shoulders.
3. Lock your hips.
4. Attempt to raise the defender up with the force of your drive.
5. Drive the defender backwards and maintain contact with him.

Follow-Through

1. Maintain a wide base as you drive your opponent.
2. Use short, choppy steps.
3. Try to turn your opponent away from the point of attack. If you cannot prevent the defender from getting to the ball, try to drive him past the point of attack.
4. If you lose contact, do not grab the defender. It is far better to have him make the tackle than it is to get a holding penalty. Also, remember that blocking from behind is not clipping in the free blocking zone.
5. Desire is the most important element in blocking, You are in a fight and you *must* win!

ADDITIONAL ONE-ON-ONE BLOCKING TECHNIQUES FOR THE RUNNING GAME

Gap Block

1. Your first step must be parallel with the line of scrimmage, not into it.
2. Your main objective is to stop penetration and drive the defender down the line.
3. You must get your head in front of the defender's belt buckle.
4. As you slip your head in front of the defender's belt, strike a shoulder—forearm-blow into his hip. Keep your "flipper" extended and parallel to the ground.
5. Keep a wide base and drive the defender down the line.
6. Figure 9-1 illustrates gap blocking techniques.

Figure 9-1

Wrong!	Right!	Correct First Step
Guard steps into the line. He will be unable to get his head in front.	Guard steps parallel to the line of scrimmage. He will be able to get his head in front of the defender.	

Blocking "Inside"

1. If the defender is aligned in the gap, utilize gap blocking techniques. The following coaching points should be used when the defender is aligned *on* the next offensive lineman to your inside.
2. Assuming that your block is not the drive block of a double-team your first step should be at the down hand of the defender that you intend to block (double-team drive blocking techniques will be covered in another section).
3. If there is a player aligned on you and he slants to your inside, lock onto him and drive him to the inside (Figure 9-2A).
4. The remaining techniques of blocking inside are identical to the gap block.
5. The principles of blocking inside also apply when you are assigned to block Linebacker. An additional point should also be mentioned in this situation. If the linebacker that you are assigned to block "disappears" because you get jammed up by a defensive lineman, continue in your intended direction until you find a different-colored jersey to block (Figure 9-2B).

Figure 9-2

9-2A

9-2B

In this Slant master call, the tackle is assigned to block Linebacker. As he steps to do this, the end slants inside. The tackle will now lock onto the end. The tight end is assigned to block inside, but when the outside linebacker slants inside, the tight end locks on to him. The pulling guard will thus trap the inside linebacker.

In this Punch master call, the tackle is assigned to block Linebacker, but when he gets jammed up by the defensive end, he continues inside and blocks the backside linebacker. In this situation, the backside guard will pick up the unblocked frontside linebacker as he pulls through the hole.

Reach Block

1. You will use a reach block when you are attempting to block a defender who is aligned in your outside gap.
2. Your first step should be parallel to the line, with your near foot.
3. As you step, drive your inside arm out and past the defender. The inside arm should be thrown in an uppercut manner.
4. As your inside arm passes the defender, scramble on all fours, attempting to turn the defender to the inside away from the point of attack.

Reverse Scramble Block

1. This is a great change of pace versus a defender who is a good "head reader."
2. Assuming that the play is to your right, you should start this block by doing everything that you normally would if the play was to your left—step with your left foot, strike a right forearm flipper into the defender, etc.
3. As the defender reacts to your head and fights pressure, drop to all fours and swing your hips around so that your right hip is in contact with the defender's left leg. As you execute this maneuver, try to make yourself "bigger," by fully extending your arms and raising your hips as high as possible.
4. From this position, begin crabbing the defender away from the direction of the play.

Downfield Block

1. Same techniques as drive blocking a linebacker.
2. Before you throw the block, station yourself in a position that will enable you to step on the defender's feet. If you throw the block any sooner, you will end up lunging at the man, missing him and landing flat on your face.

SPECIAL TECHNIQUES FOR PULLING LINEMEN

Pulling

1. Your first step should be made with your near foot. This step should be a quick jab-step about 6 inches long.

2. If you are required to belly back during your first few steps of pulling, you should vigorously whip your near forearm and head to the side as you take your first step. In this instance, your first step must be slightly deeper than parallel to the line. You should gradually gain depth on your second and third steps and then adjust your course to the reaction of the defender that you are assigned to block.

3. If you are not required to belly back, your first step should be toward the line. When pulling "into the line," it is not necessary to vigorously whip your near forearm to the side. Instead, you should collapse your back knee and pivot on your back foot. This will insure that you take a short jab-step with your near foot.

4. As you take your first step, you should quickly focus your eyes on your intended target.

5. It is important that you stay low as you pull.

6. As you are pulling, if you "feel" a defender penetrating through the line, stop and block him. Never pass by one defender to block another because the defender that you pass by is sure to make the tackle deep in the backfield.

Blocking Techniques for Pulling Linemen (Figure 9-3)

Figure 9-3

This is the standard trap block. The trapper pulls into the line and blocks the defender with his right shoulder if he is pulling to the right and his left shoulder if he is pulling to the left.

This technique is used by the tackle when he is assigned to Fill. The tackle will reach-block any defender in his gap, or a defender shading the outside shoulder of the guard. Otherwise, he will pull down the line and clip any defender who penetrates. If no one penetrates, the tackle will turn upfield when he gets to the B gap. This is used for Power and Punch master calls.

Figure 9-3 (Cont'd.)

This technique is used when a backside lineman is assigned to pull and lead. In this instance, the guard will pull into the line and turn upfield when he is close enough to touch the drive blocker (TE). As he turns upfield, the guard's first priority is to block any linebacker who is shuffling down the line, close to the hole. If there are none, the guard will continue downfield.

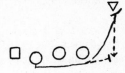

Used when the frontside guard is assigned to pull and lead (Quick Pitch or Stampede). The guard will belly back and locate the secondary defender assigned containment. If this defender comes up quickly, the guard will trap him with a right shoulder block. If the defender stays back, the guard will block him downfield using a left shoulder block.

The curl block is used versus a Split-4 scraping linebacker. It can also be used versus gap stacks. The guard's first step should be parallel to the line thus allowing adequate clearance for the tackle. The guard should block the linebacker with his inside (left shoulder.

The frontside guard will use this technique for the sweep master call. The guard will pull parallel to the line, keeping his eyes glued to the linebacker. He will pursue the linebacker from an inside-out position. If the linebacker shoots one of the gaps, the guard will block him. If not, the guard will pull around and block the LB with his left shoulder.

The frontside guard will use this technique for Rip, Blast, Slant, Bend and Slice master calls. The guard will step into the line and block the linebacker with his outside (right) shoulder.

This technique is used by the backside guard for Gut and Sprint Draw master calls. The guard will step into the line and block the linebacker with his outside (left) shoulder.

THE DOUBLE-TEAM BLOCK

The Post Blocker

1. If the defender is playing inside shade, or head up with you, step with your inside foot and block him with your outside shoulder. Expect that the defender will slant inside. If he does, you will block him alone (Figure 9-4B and Figure 9-4C).

2. If he is playing outside shade, step with your outside foot first and scramble toward the defender on all fours. Force him to protect the "Crown Jewels." This will tie up his hands and force his hip to be extended backwards and thus make him a good target for the drive blocker.

Figure 9-4

Figure 9-4A   Figure 9-4B   Figure 9-4C

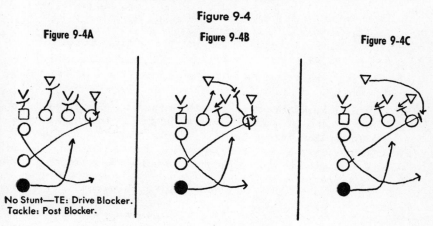

No Stunt—TE: Drive Blocker.
Tackle: Post Blocker.

The Drive Blocker

1. Step with your inside foot first.
2. Aim for the defender's near hip and block this target with an inside forearm "flipper."
3. If the defender's near hip disappears because he slants inside, continue on down the line until you find a linebacker (Figure 9-4B).
4. If there is a defender on you and he slants inside, lock onto him and block him inside (9-4C).

DROPBACK PASSING TECHNIQUES

1. Set up quickly with your shoulders square to the line.
2. Bend at the knees, but keep your back straight.
3. College and pro players are allowed to extend their arms with the palms of their hands facing the defender.

4. High school players must keep their hands closed, with their elbows and forearms close to their body.

5. Your object is to stay between the defender and the passer.

6. Wait for the defender to come to you; do not lunge at him.

7. As the defender comes toward you, college and pro players will try to get their palms on the defender's pectoral muscles. High school players will try to establish contact on the same target with the bottom sides of their fists.

8. As the defender moves laterally, shuffle with him, moving your back leg first and exerting maximum pressure with the hand that is in the direction of the defender's movements. *Example:* The defender moves to your right. Shuffle with him, moving your left foot first, and exert maximum pressure with your right arm.

9. If you start to lose the defender, you must quickly attempt to drive-block him. *Example:* The defender is moving to your right and he is starting to beat you. Quickly shoulder-block him with your left "flipper." Try to drive the defender with your left ear on his belt buckle.

10. When employing a sprint-out, or play action pass, we will use the standard drive block.

11. If the pass is a quick three-step drop, offensive linemen should set up as though it were a normal dropback pass. Just as the defender comes toward you, quickly drop down and force him to protect the "Crown Jewels." This will force the defender to keep his hands down and out of the path of the ball. Do not drop down too soon; if you do, this technique will be ineffective.

10 Coaching Combo Blocking Techniques

Although the techniques of the four combo calls were illustrated in Chapter 2, I did not discuss how to execute these techniques versus different defenses. This is one of the objectives of this brief chapter. Another objective is to provide the reader with a comprehensive checklist of when each combo call can be utilized. Some readers may wish to refer to the section entitled "Combo Calls" in Chapter 2, to refresh their memories before proceeding with this chapter.

COMBO CROSSBLOCK TECHNIQUES

We crossblock four different types of defensive sets. These are:

1. An "On" set—both linemen are covered by down linemen, or linebackers who are playing on the line of scrimmage (Figure 10-1A).
2. An "On-Over" set—One lineman is covered by a down lineman and the other is covered by a linebacker who is playing off the line (Figure 10-1B).
3. A "Gap-Stack" set—A linebacker is stacked behind a down lineman who is aligned in a gap (Figure 10-1C).
4. A "Stack" set—A linebacker is stacked behind a down lineman who is aligned on an offensive lineman (Figure 10-1D).

Figure 10-1

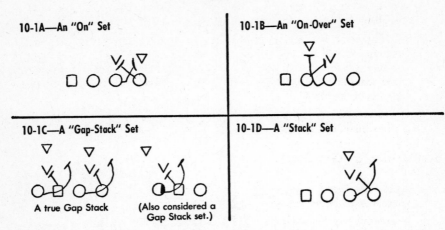

10-1A—An "On" Set

10-1B—An "On-Over" Set

10-1C—A "Gap-Stack" Set

A true Gap Stack

(Also considered a Gap Stack set.)

10-1D—A "Stack" Set

Before we discuss the techniques of crossblocking, it should be noted that whenever two offensive linemen crossblock, neither lineman goes first. They both go at the same time. One of the players, however, must yield the right of way to the other. This is accomplished by adjusting the steps of each player to insure adequate clearance.

Crossblocking an "On" Set

1. We crossblock an "On" set to divide two defenders at the point of attack. *Example:* When employing a Quick master call to engineer an off-tackle play, the FSE and FST crossblock.

2. When the right tackle and tight end (Fig. 10-1A) execute a crossblock, the tight end will step directly at the defensive end's down hand and block this defender with a right shoulder block. It is important that the blocker keep his right ear on the defender's belt buckle as he drives him down the line.

3. The tackle will step parallel to the line, thus yielding the right of way to the tight end. The tackle will block the outside linebacker with a right shoulder block.

4. If the defensive end were to slant to the inside, it would be impossible for the tight end to block him. It is thus important to note that offensive linemen should not call crossblocks versus "On" sets that frequently stunt or slant.

Crossblocking an "On-Over" Set

1. We crossblock this set to divide the two defenders at the point of attack. *Example:* When employing a Quick Right master call for a play directed at the B gap, the FSG and FST call a crossblock (Figure 10-1B). Another reason to call the same crossblock might be to confuse the inside linebacker's read in an attempt to slow down his pursuit. In this instance, the play would be "Quick Left," thus making the right tackle the BST and the right guard the BSG.

2. When executing this crossblock, the right guard must cheat up slightly toward the line and step directly at the defensive end's down hand with his right foot. The guard will block the defender with his left shoulder.

3. It is important that the tackle's first step is deep and away from the line, otherwise he will not allow adequate clearance for the guard. As he pulls around, he will block the linebacker with his right shoulder. The tackle should expect that the linebacker will react to the guard's block by jab-stepping in the direction of the block.

4. Unlike a crossblock versus an "On" set, a crossblock versus an "On-Over" set is an excellent call against a slanting or stunting defense.

Crossblocking a "Gap Stack" Set

1. A crossblock versus a gap stack is used by both frontside and backside linemen to seal off defensive pursuit.

2. Most teams that utilize gap stack alignments do so for the purpose of employing scraping linebackers. Such teams seldom slant their down linemen. Instead, they use their linemen to shoot the gaps (Figure 10-2A). Some teams, on the other hand, do attempt to slant their down linemen (Figure 10-2B). When confronted by a team that slants their down linemen, an offensive team should only employ backside, gap stack crossblocks. Attempting to crossblock a frontside, guard-tackle gap stack, for example, would prove to be devastating, since it is impossible for the offensive tackle to block a gap defender who slants to the inside.

3. When executing a frontside crossblock between the right guard and tackle, the tackle will step at the down hand of the defensive lineman and block him with his right shoulder.

4. The right guard will pull around and block the linebacker with his left shoulder.

Figure 10-2

10-2A

10-2B

Crossblocking a Stack

1. This call can be made by both frontside and backside linemen to seal off defensive pursuit. *Example:* Power right—the right tackle and tight end call a crossblock versus a 5-3 Stack (Figure 10-1D).

2. The tight end steps with his inside foot and executes a right shoulder block on the down defender.

3. The tackle steps slightly deeper than parallel to the line and pulls around and blocks the tandem linebacker with his left shoulder.

4. A crossblock should not be called versus stunting stack defenses. Instead, a Pop call should be made.

A COACH'S COMPLETE CHECKLIST FOR COMBO CROSSBLOCKS

ASE & AST	AST & ASG	ASG & C	C & BSG	BSG & BST
Quick Off-Tackle: 3-4 Strong Gap Stack Pro 4-3 College 4-3 5-3 Stack Tight 6 6-5 *Quick Y:* 5-3 Stack 6-5	*Power:* Weak Gap Stack Eagle College 4-3 4-3 Eagle *Quick Off-Tackle:* Split-4 Weak Gap Stack Eagle College 4-3 4-3 Eagle *Quick Y:* (Same defenses as Quick) *Quick Inside:* Split-4 Weak Gap Stack Eagle College 4-3 4-3 Eagle 3-4	*Quick Inside:* College 4-3 4-3 Eagle	*Quick Off-Tackle:* Weak Gap Stack College 4-3 4-3 Eagle *Quick Y:* (Same defenses as Quick) *Slant:* (Same as above) *Bend* (Same as above) *Slice:* Same as above *Rip:* (Same as above) *Quick Inside:* (Same as above) *Veer:* (Same as above) *Outside Ice:* 6-5 College 4-3 4-3 Eagle Pro 4-3 Wide 6 Tight 6 *Inside Ice:* (Same as above) *Sweep:* Weak Gap Stack *Y Sweep:* Weak Gap Stack *Packer:* Weak Gap Stack	*Quick Off-Tackle* 3-4 Strong Gap Stack 5-3 5-3 Stack *Quick Y:* (Same defenses as Quick) *Slant:* (Same as above) *Bend:* (Same as above) *Slice:* (Same as above) *Rip:* (Same as above) *Inside Quick:* (Same as above) *Veer:* (Same as above) *Outside Ice:* (Same as above) *Inside Ice:* 3-4 5-3 Stack

SCOOP TECHNIQUES

This call is made between the backside guard and center only. No other players will call scoop. Scoop is only used versus odd defenses (3-4, 5-3 and 5-3 Stack). The purpose of scoop is to cut off backside pursuit. When applied to the 3-4 defense, the techniques of scoop would be as follows:

GUARD: Step parallel to the line of scrimmage and block the nose tackle with your outside shoulder if he slants into the backside A gap. If he doesn't slant, pull around and block the backside linebacker with your outside shoulder. *Note:* If a stack linebacker (5-3, or 5-3 Stack), stunts into the backside A gap, you would also block him.

CENTER: Step for the outside foot of the nose and block him with your far shoulder if he charges straight at you or into the attackside A gap. (*Far shoulder:* If you step with your right foot, your left shoulder is your far shoulder.) If the nose slants into the backside A gap, block the linebacker with your far shoulder.

A COACH'S COMPLETE CHECKLIST FOR SCOOP COMBO CALLS

The backside guard and the center may call scoop in the following situations:

1. Slant: 3-4, 5-3
2. Bend: 3-4, 5-3, 5-3 Stack
3. Slice: 3-4, 5-3, 5-3 Stack
4. Rip: 3-4, 5-3, 5-3 Stack
5. Quick: 3-4

ZONE TECHNIQUES

Zone is an attackside call that can be used versus both odd and even defenses. The call enables offensive linemen to block stunting defenses. The following techniques would be used by the frontside guard and tackle to block a 3-4 defensive end and inside linebacker:

GUARD: Step with your outside foot and block the defensive end with your far shoulder if he slants into the B gap. If the end does not slant, run through the B gap and block the linebacker with your far shoulder. Note that the main difference between scoop and zone is that zone does not employ a pulling technique.

TACKLE: Step with your outside foot and block the end with your far shoulder if he charges straight ahead or slants into the C gap. If the end slants into the B gap, block the linebacker with your far shoulder.

A COACH'S COMPLETE CHECKLIST FOR ZONE COMBO CALLS

The attackside guard and tackle may call zone in the following situations:

1. Quick (Inside, or off-tackle): 3-4

The attackside guard and center may call zone in the following situations:

1. Quick (Inside, or off-tackle): College 4-3, 4-3
2. Quick Y: College 4-3, 4-3

The attackside tackle and center may call zone in the following situations:

1. Blast: 4-3, College 4-3
2. Slant: 4-3, College 4-3

POP TECHNIQUES

Pop is an attackside call that is used to attack stack, guard stack and tandem defenses. The call enables the offense to block stunts. The following techniques would be used by the frontside guard and tackle to block a guard stack set.

GUARD: Step straight at the defender playing on you and block him with your inside shoulder if he charges straight at you, or into the A gap. If the defender charges into the B gap, block the linebacker with your inside shoulder.

TACKLE: Step with your inside foot and extend your inside arm directly at the outside shoulder of the defensive lineman. If this defender slants into the B gap, block him with your far shoulder. If he doesn't slant into the B gap, push the defender into the guard, using the fist of your inside arm (college and pro players can use the palm of their hand to do this), and then quickly block the linebacker with your inside shoulder.

A COACH'S COMPLETE CHECKLIST FOR POP COMBO CALLS

ASE & AST	AST & ASG	ASG & C	ASG & C (Cont'd.)
Power: 5-3 Stack 6-5	*Quick (Inside and Off-Tackle):* Split-4	*G Punch:* 5-3 5-3 Stack	*Trap:* 5-3 5-3 Stack
G Punch: Same as above	*Quick Y:* Same as above	*Power:* Same as above	*T Trap:* Same as above
Quick Off-Tackle: Same as above	*Veer:* Same as above	*Quick Off-Tackle* Same as above	*Y Trap:* Same as above
Bend: Same as above		*Quick Y:* Same as above	*Gut:* Same as above
Slice: Same as above		*Quick* Inside Same as above	*Outside Ice:* Same as above
		Veer: Same as above	*Inside Ice:* 5-3 Stack

11

How to Put Radar
Blocking into Action

HOW TO INSTALL RADAR BLOCKING INTO ANY OFFEN-
SIVE SYSTEM

Although coaches vary greatly in the specifics, there are probably only three basic systems of organizing and communicating offensive plays. To illustrate my explanations of how Radar Blocking can be installed into these three systems, I have diagrammed five commonly used running plays, along with a very simple method of hole numbering (Figures 11-1 A, B, C, D, E and F).

The first system of organizing and communicating offensive plays uses nomenclature rather than numbers. In this system, plays are referred to as: Power, Sweep, Dive, etc. If two different running backs are used for the same play (Figures 11-1A and E), it then becomes necessary to number the running backs. Assuming that the quarterback is number 1, the fullback 3, the halfback 4 and the wingback 2, Figure 11-1A would be referred to as 40 power and Figure 11-1E would be referred to as 20 power. This system easily integrates with Radar blocking because each play can be given the same nomenclature as the master call used to engineer it.

The second system numbers both the backs and the intended hole through which they run. Figure 11-1A would thus be referred to as a 46. When integrating Radar Blocking with this system, a coach need only add the name of the master call to the two-digit number. This would make Figure 11-1A a 46 Power, Figure 11-1B a 48 Stampede, etc. An added advantage of this system is that it now becomes possible to utilize the same backfield action with different master calls. Figure 11-1D, for example, uses the same backfield action as a 46 Power, but because it utilizes Punch blocking, it is therefore referred to as a 46 Punch.

The last system organizes plays into series. Because Figures 11-1 A, B C and D are all characterized by the same initial backfield action, all four of these plays would thus be grouped into a series. Let's call this the 20 series. This system also utilizes a two-digit number. The first digit designates the series number and the second digit designates the hole that is attacked.

Figure 11-1

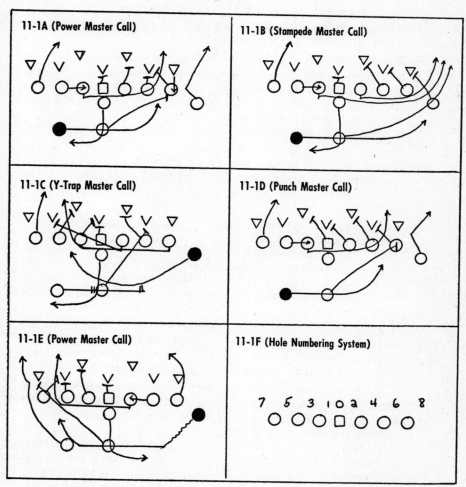

Radar blocking is integrated into this system in the same exact manner as it was in the preceding system. The plays in Figure 11-1 would thus be referred to as:

A— 26 Power

B— 28 Stampede

C— 23 Y Trap

D— 26 Punch

E— This play would not be grouped into this series since it has a different initial backfield action.

HOW TO COACH RADAR BLOCKING
UTILIZING THE PROPER TEACHING PROGRESSION

1. First teach linemen their proper rule blocking terminology.

2. Next, teach the blocking rules for the specific master calls that you have chosen. Introduce one master call at a time. Try to limit your total number of master calls. Remember, you can employ multiple backfield actions with a single master call. From my own personal experience, I have found that most players are capable of learning about ten total master calls.

3. Right from the beginning, practice your master calls versus multiple defenses. This will force your players to learn their blocking rules. If you only practice your offense against one or two different defenses, most players will not memorize their rules. They will simply learn their assignments for those one or two defenses.

4. Next, begin practicing combo techniques. As your players become proficient at these techniques, you can gradually begin to integrate your combo calls with your master calls. Do not expect that your players will be able to immediately combo multiple defenses, or even memorize the specific defenses that can be comboed with each master call. This involves too much memorization and recognition skill and is thus impossible. You must teach players to combo one defense at a time.

5. In spring football and during the preseason, we attempt to teach our players their combo calls versus two or three defenses. We keep things simple and just try to establish a sound learning base. As we progress into the season, we prepare a weekly checklist of the combo calls that we expect to use.

6. At game time, if we are confronted by a "surprise" defense, we may not immediately know how to combo it, but everyone will immediately know their base assignment for every master call, because they have memorized their inclusive rule assignments. If our opponents are stunting a lot, some of our master calls will be vulnerable to these stunts because of our inability to combo the "surprise," but our offense will still function well. We will simply avoid using those master calls that rely on combo calls and base our attack on master calls that do not utilize combo calls. Once we figure out what our opponent is

doing and determine the best combo calls against these tactics, we will relate this information to our players. It may take us until half time to accomplish this, but so what? Our offense hasn't been hurting. We were not vulnerable to the "surprise." The "surprise" merely limited our play selection for a period of time.

7. In selecting master calls, it is thus important to select three or four master calls that do not require combo calls. These master calls should engineer your base running plays. In this way, you will never leave yourself vulnerable to a "surprise" defense.

8. I personally believe that high school, frosh and J.V. coaches should use offensive systems that are constructed of master calls that do not heavily rely on a lot of combo calls. At these levels, I would prefer to keep things extremely simple. Wait until a player gets to the varsity before you teach him to combo block. There are enough master calls for frosh and J.V. coaches to select, that are not dependent upon combo calls, yet enable them to engineer their attack versus any defensive set, or stunt. My philosophy is to teach young players sound blocking fundamentals, utilize an extremely simple offensive system and WIN! Winning is a habit, and this habit should be nurtured as soon as possible.

9. Coaches who employ option type offenses (the wishbone, the veer, etc.), will argue that it is impossible for them to engineer their attack without using a multitude of combo techniques—and they are correct. Teaching option football, however, is much different than teaching most other systems. First of all, option linemen do not have to learn as many different kinds of blocking schemes as linemen in other systems. Furthermore, most option attacks will only utilize about four or five total master calls. As a result, option coaches will place far greater emphasis on the combo aspect of Radar Blocking than will coaches of other systems. This is true even at frosh and J.V. levels.

Index